Caring for

DOVER's POOR

by

Derek Leach

Riverdale Publications, 24 Riverdale, River, Dover CT17 0QX

Published in 2006 by Riverdale Publications
24 Riverdale, River, Dover CT17 0QX

ISBN 0 9536166 6 5

Printed in England by A. R. Adams (Printers) Ltd.,
The Printing House, Dour Street, Dover, CT16 1EW

CONTENTS

River House, formerly River Workhouse – drawing by Jane Leach

INTRODUCTION

The proud and ancient town of Dover has a fascinating history dating from Roman times. Occupying such an important strategic position so close to the continent, it has played various important roles in the history of the country. It has served as a launching pad over the centuries for our armies on the way to invade, or in more recent times to liberate, Europe. It has also been the main conduit for travellers to and from mainland Europe and, until the advent of air travel, was also the gateway used by British and foreign royalty. Nicknamed Hellfire Corner, the town and its White Cliffs epitomised Britain's defiant spirit during two world wars in the 20th century.

The town still has some incredible buildings, both below and above ground, to remind modern tourists of its glorious past: extensive Roman remains, including the Pharos and the Painted House, Saxon remains, the Norman castle, the Maison Dieu founded in 1203, the remains of Dover Priory, extensive Napoleonic fortifications and the harbour, dating from medieval times.

Over the centuries, Dover's story has been well told by various historians, both local and national, but one aspect has perhaps been neglected or overlooked: the plight of its poor. Whilst we are familiar with Dover's leading townsmen and their exploits, what do we know about the poor folk? Not much, since they did little of note, although there are references to organisations which cared for them. Until attitudes changed in the 20th century, the poor were often detested, usually feared and almost always regarded with shame.

The poor are always with us, it is said, and this is still true today. This book attempts to describe the problem of poverty in Dover over the centuries and how the authorities, both religious and secular, as well as certain individuals responded to it.

Derek Leach, April 2006.

Chapter 1

MEDIEVAL TIMES

By the 12th century Dover's massive castle overshadowed the town and port. The town enjoyed a privileged status as one of the Cinque Ports and was already an important point of embarkation and for trade with the continent with a thriving fishing community centred around the then haven by (old) St. James' Church. An annual fair, dating from 1160, was held in the churchyard of St. Martin Le Grand. Following the move of the canons from St. Martin Le Grand to the new St. Martin's Priory in the twelfth century, St. Martin Le Grand became a parish church and, unusually, also housed the altars of both St. Nicholas and St. John the Baptist parishes. Within the town were also the parishes of St. Mary, St. James and St. Peter. Close by was St. Radigund's Abbey at Bradsole.

Dover had suffered mixed fortunes as a result of war, both with France and internal strife. A consequence of Simon de Montfort's rebellion had been some loss of autonomy. However, the murder of Thomas Becket in Canterbury Cathedral in 1170 combined with a virtual monopoly of passenger traffic across the Channel meant that Dover's economy gained considerably from the steady flow of pilgrims needing bed and board en route to and from Canterbury.

The role of the religious hospital in medieval England was researched in recent times from surviving records by Dr. Sheila Sweetinburgh, including the part played by Dover's religious houses. This provides a valuable starting point for a study of how the poor of Dover were cared at that time and the developments from then to the present day.

An impression of Dover Castle in the 12th century by J. Flavin

St. Bartholomew's Hospital

St. Bartholomew's Hospital was founded on what is now known as Chapel Hill in Buckland in 1141 by two monks from St. Martin's Priory, named Osborne and Godwin, using funds from goods left them by their parents. Its lands extended down the slopes of the hill to the river where St. Bartholomew's Chapel was situated. Apparently no windows of the hospital looked outwards. Whilst catering for poor pilgrims initially, it soon became a leper hospital as well, housing 20 men and women long term. The men would work on the farm land of the hospital whilst the women were employed indoors. All had to obey the rules of the house, which survive in the Bodleian Library at Oxford. These included praying for the monks of Dover Priory, loving the other residents, attending chapel daily, wearing the prescribed habit and staying within the precincts of the hospital. Men were not to tap on the women's dormitory at night, nor play pranks or make assignations. Inmates were pledged to a life of sobriety and usefulness, but all were allowed to beg. The Warden was head of the house and nobody left without his permission. The usual diet consisted of pork, barley and beer with some extras on church festival days. The hospital was relatively poor, living on the profits from the farming, but there were benefactors, although few locally. It was supported to some extent by the townspeople indirectly via tolls and fish tithes

St. Richard of Chichester

2

*Hubert de Burgh
as portrayed in the 1908 Dover Pageant*

paid to Dover Priory and also received the profit from the annual St. Bartholomew's Fair. The hospital did not cater for the destitute, since there was a modest entry fee of half a mark i.e. 13s. 4d., payable to the warden, 4d payable to each of the residents plus a fee for the porter; half a resident's goods had to be left to the hospital upon death. The destitute, whilst not allowed as residents, were not ignored completely, however, since they were given dole at the gate. In addition there was an annual distribution of ale to the poor, thanks to a bequest from a lady in exchange for prayers to be said for her soul. In 1252 Bishop Richard of Chichester offered a 20 day indulgence to all who supported the poor at the hospital. 1511 is thought to be the last year that lepers lived in St. Bartholomew's. When it was suppressed by Henry VIII in 1536 as part of the Dissolution of the Monasteries it possessed 159 acres of land around Dover, 24 houses and two mills, which had provided its income.

Maison Dieu

In 1203 Hubert de Burgh founded St. Mary's Hospital – the Maison Dieu – outside the town walls to provide hospitality for poor pilgrims and the poor of the town. He and subsequent benefactors fulfilled their duty to God by giving alms to the poor and in so doing hoped to gain eternal life for their souls. One of the hospital's acts of mercy was to provide Christian burials for the local poor and for sick pilgrims who did not reach Canterbury. This relieved the town of its responsibility. St. Edmund's Chapel, which still stands today was built by the monks of Maison Dieu in their cemetery for the poor and was consecrated by St. Richard of Chichester in 1253. Offerings to

St. Edmund's Chapel

St. Richard of Chichester who died at the hospital in 1253 plus income from donated lands provided funds to support the charitable activities of the hospital.

14th and 15th centuries

During the 14th century with a lack of manufacturing industry, except for a few craftsmen, there was a heavy reliance on cross Channel passenger trade. Many families stayed for one generation only, although there was a small core of long-standing families both rich and poor. Like the rest of the country, the people suffered from regular outbreaks of the plague.

Religious houses had little support from the townspeople. The Maison Dieu's work for the poor and pilgrims was affected by the cost of having to provide hospitality for the monarch and his entourage as well as having to find somewhere to live for aged royal servants. The Priory, where the king had his own chamber, also had to provide hospitality for royal visitors, papal officials and churchmen.

The old silted-up harbour by old St. James' Church was abandoned by the end of the 13th century following a cliff fall. Ships were forced to beach on the western side of Dover Bay where some shelter was provided by the small promontory of Archcliffe. This became the new harbour. In the 15th century, with this harbour threatened by the drift of shingle from the east blocking the harbour mouth, Henry VIII funded some remedial work which was only partially successful. The project stimulated the economy for a time by providing work, but there was an increasing number of poor folk.

Dover's leading citizens appear to have had little interest in supporting the needy either during their lives or following their deaths via donations or bequests to the religious houses, believing perhaps that establishing and maintaining the corporation's almshouse, founded in the late 15th century, was sufficient. The mayor and jurats were remarkably tolerant or disinterested, merely watching for vagabonds and occasionally giving small sums to the destitute. Vagrants unable to work were sent back to their birthplace and those capable of work were severely dealt with;

Ruins of St. Martin Le Grand

4

punishment ranged from whipping, loss of ears to hanging. Care of the poor was a religious duty after all and it was up to religious houses to make distributions of food to the poor appeared to be the official attitude.

The Dissolution

St. Bartholomew's was dissolved between 1539 and 1540 and Henry VIII gave its buildings, the chapel and lands to John Bowle, the Mayor and inn keeper of the Lion, for life. He destroyed it. By 1558 when he died no buildings other than a

An impression of the Maison Dieu c.1800

Maison Dieu prior to 1834

5

St. Martin's Priory – a farm c. 1850

Gateway of St. Martin's Priory

fulling mill were left standing. What happened to the inmates is not known. Large parts of St. Martin Le Grand and the Priory were also destroyed at the Dissolution. By the 16th century the grand Maison Dieu establishment was reduced to the humble task of providing temporary lodgings for poor soldiers, sailors and passengers. When it was surrendered in 1544 its furnishings were way past their best, but there was plenty of silver and livestock! It had almost ceased to function and had virtually become the king's property with its land used as a building yard for harbour works by its master, Sir John Thompson. It then became officially Crown property.

When Henry VIII closed Dover Priory, the Maison Dieu and St. Bartholomew's Hospital, the tradition of such institutions caring for the needy ended. To compensate, the King required churchwardens and two others in every parish to collect for the poor every Sunday to avoid the need for begging. This was observed in Dover's St. Mary's and St. James' parishes. There were some unpleasant disputes between the governors of the almshouse charity and guardians of the poor of St. Mary's Parish regarding who should benefit from the charity. St. Mary's complained that they were frequently burdened by so many casual poor that the charity should provide for.

It can be seen that by the end of the medieval period with the demise of the religious houses the King saw the need for some replacement system to care for the poor, however crudely. The responsibility was laid upon every parish. This became the blueprint until the 20th century with the government providing the legal framework and the parish operating the system locally.

Dover Priory refectory

Chapter 2

ECONOMY AND SOCIETY 1509-1640

Mary Dixon in her 1992 doctorate thesis, entitled *Economy and Society in Dover 1509 to 1640*, provides a fascinating insight into Dover society's treatment of both the 'deserving' and 'undeserving' poor from her exhaustive study of the surviving town and court records of the period.

Population and employment

For much of the period Dover was a small market town with a decaying harbour, although Henry VIII's harbour improvements did bring work and money to the town, attracting merchants and foreign trade. The local historian, Revd. John Lyon, in 1564 records that there were 358 houses in Dover of which 29 were empty. By the 17th century there were 566 men between 16 and 60 years, of these 139 were described as mariners, which included fishing, piloting, carrying, ferrying, harbour work, curing and selling fish, supplying oakum, smuggling, piracy and theft! Between 1570 and 1670 the town's population was probably between two and three thousand. The rich became richer and the poor remained poor or poorer. The sea provided much of the work: fishing, ferrying goods and passengers from ship to shore (in the absence of a deep water entrance to the harbour or suitable jetty). Often the same person would be engaged in all these occupations. Much of the work was seasonal. A man could eke out a living by fishing in the autumn, carting in the summer and at the same time graze a couple of sheep. Shipbuilding on the beach was another occupation – William Yeames

Shipbuilding on the beach, 1792

who died in 1694 left a shipyard worth nearly £400. Woolcombing took place in the area now called Woolcomber Street, lime from the chalk cliff face was exported to France and the Low Countries and by 1654 papermaking had commenced at Buckland. It was the 17th century which saw a movement of population from the town to the reclaimed land of the Pier District to the west.

Wages for harbour works in the 1530s ranged from 5d. to 8d. a day for masons, sawyers and carpenters whilst labourers earned 4d. and the paymaster received 4s. By the early 17th century labourers were earning 1s. a day. Throughout this period the corporation paid bakers one shilling a dozen for loaves.

Woolcomber Street - photograph by Amos & Amos c.1900

Buckland paper mill in 1770

Museum model of Dover Harbour and town in 1595

In addition to its essential role as the nearest port to the continent, catering for many travellers, both religious and secular, the prime function of the town and its tradesmen from 1500 to 1700 was to provide goods and services to its own population and the surrounding countryside, which supplied the Dover market with grain, meat and tallow. The expansion of foreign trade in the 17th century meant more ships to supply with provisions. Local wealth no longer came chiefly from the fields outside the town, but from storehouses, malthouses, brewhouses, quays and wagons carrying goods to and from the ships.

Dover's growing economic prosperity depended, however, for the most part upon factors outside its control – weather, tides, disease, piracy, war and government decisions such as to improve the harbour and later to transfer its control from the town to James I's commissioners. The economic expansion meant that the population increased, which led to overcrowding and disorder and the attraction to the town of vagrants and paupers. The gap widened between rich and poor. War and disease contributed to problems caused by increasing population, rising prices and falls in wages in the late 16th and early 17th centuries. Even the harbour works of the 1580s and 1590s, which brought work and men to Dover, also resulted in the need for temporary relief.

Disease

Sickness and death were common. Throughout these years the people of Dover suffered outbreaks of bubonic plague with high mortality rates in 1559, 1603, 1625/6 1637/40 and 1665/6, which was also the last epidemic. Closely packed streets and the habit of keeping all the occupiers of a dwelling shut in once any member of the family caught the plague did not help. Tuberculosis was a common cause of death exacerbated by bad air and poor ventilation in the tiny hovels. Insanitary conditions meant that typhus and typhoid also flourished and smallpox and influenza took their toll.

Attitude of the civic authority to the poor

With the disappearance of most monks and priests the protestant ruling group took upon themselves the moral as well as the civic authority, widening the gulf between governors and governed. Over these years a haphazard but personal relief system gave way to a more impersonal rule-governed system, keeping the needy out of sight.

The corporation's first duty was to care for the long-established inhabitants of the town, both poor and free. At times of hardship rents were written off and casual employment was found whenever possible for long term poor inhabitants. Sometimes the rents of temporarily, disabled poor were paid and on one occasion the wife and children were assisted financially when the husband went to prison for beating up his wife.

Treatment of the homeless poor, such as beggars, runaway servants and apprentices however young, unmarried couples living together and 'harlots' became more censorious in the early 17th century, since they were felt to be offences against the orderly, godly family. There was some alleviation, however, for extreme old age and pregnancy within marriage. Other people genuinely seeking work were sometimes merely admonished and sent away rather than whipped.

At the same time those who might bring benefit to the town were not only allowed in but were sometimes granted freemanship at a discount.

Corporation's relief of the poor

From 1560s and 70s there was greater intervention and increased spending by the corporation on care for the needy and prevention of sickness, suggesting a growing poverty problem, or perhaps the corporation taking more responsibility for the impotent poor – coinciding, perhaps, with the much reduced role of the church following the Dissolution in the 1530s and 1540s.

Poor relief payments by the corporation were occasional and mainly to cover emergencies. Payments started in 1550 at less than £1 a year in total, but by 1578 the annual cost had risen to over £8. Between 1553 and 1576 there were a few payments mainly to long standing and respectable inhabitants – the impotent, deserving poor. One such man, John Meye, received annual amounts for clothing in old age and even 4d. for being trimmed by a barber. The corporation also showed loyalty to those who had served it well – the town sergeant from 1561 until his terminal illness in 1574 received payments during his sickness and after his death his widow received money. There were nine payments between 1565 and 1570, including one to a mariner who had 'lost his ship' and to two foundlings. In 1566 payments in kind of 500 faggots of wood were provided for the poor. Emergency payments for burials, such as those of unknowns found 'cast upon the shore', varied from 2d. for somebody who died suddenly at the Pier to 6s. 5d. for another who had some standing in the town. Between 1585 and 1588 the town spent £5 18s. 2d. on food, board and transport or the burial of poor soldiers 'from beyond the seas.' By the early 1600s the corporation's total expenditure upon its own poor, the transient poor and burials was over £20 a year.

The peak period for relief was 1588 to 1614. There was a local custom of giving doles of bread to the poor at civic festivities such as the annual coronation day celebrations, but this ceased in 1607 when it was replaced by the corporation providing cheap rye and wheat. Some expenditure was due to infectious diseases. In 1602 the corporation paid a butcher 17s. 6d. for meat for those sick with the plague. Women were paid for caring for the sick and searching the bodies and there were payments for the burial of plague victims.

Legislative changes in 1598 and 1610 meant that little was spent thereafter on the transient poor, which, combined with different ways of caring for Dover's own poor, resulted in annual expenditure dropping to less than £1 by 1620. Whilst the town's expenditure on poor relief in the town's accounts declined, expenditure continued via the almshouse, the overseers of the poor and their accounts.

The corporation bought a dwelling in Cowgate Street in 1610 for use as a House of Correction where poor people could be set to work, although it did not open until 1613. £10 was spent on the conversion. It was agreed that James Hilles, a hemp dresser, would supply the inmates and all other poor persons of the town who could not provide work for themselves with materials, meat and drink at his cost and make 'the best use of their labour.' He was given an allowance for workers under 12 who could not earn their food. Care of children in private homes stopped and the overseer of the House of Correction was given an allowance for keeping children under 12.

Children

The first recorded payment for keeping a bastard at corporation expense was in 1577 and for the next thirty or forty years payments for the care of bastards, orphans and foundlings were the most common expenses incurred.

Between 1578 and 1618 orphans and bastard children were placed in the care of townsfolk at corporation expense of a shilling a week or 1s. 2d. if nursing. Up to seven needy women were being used at any one time. Some children were removed from the corporation's hands permanently in return for a one off payment of about £1.

As soon as the children were old enough they were taken on as apprentices. Some were badly treated. Those who ran away and later caught were punished with a public whipping in the town hall, unless the master pleaded for mercy. There were many examples of orphans and children of widowed mothers being placed as apprentices by the corporation in return for some favour to the master, such as a tax reduction or free entry into freemanship. A detailed apprentice's indenture dated 1583 lists the conditions to be observed: to preserve the master's secrets; to keep his commandments; not to fornicate in or out of the master's house; not to hurt his master; not to haunt any victualling or tippling houses unless about the master's business; not to play any unlawful games; not to waste, spend, lend or consume any of the master's goods; not to absent himself from the master's service by day or night; to behave as a true and faithful servant and apprentice should do. For his part, the master promised to teach and instruct and to allow the apprentice meat, drink, hose, shoes and everything necessary for the craft, but also to correct and chastise as necessary! Seamanship absorbed the majority of the poorer children.

Bread and fish

With increasing sea trade maltsters and merchants began to play a major role in the town's economy, but also added to the condition of the poor, since they bought up much of the local harvest for export. The corporation had to intervene and required the maltsters to bring some barley to the town market and sell it for 16s. a quarter and in 1597 the corporation undertook to provide 100 quarters of wheat and rye between April and midsummer to save the poor from starvation. In 1604, empowered by the Privy Council, they took 4 quarters (of a hundred-weight) from every 20 for export from Dover and sold it to the poor at 20s. a quarter and to others at 24s. a quarter. The corporation was in debt in the 1620s and, with little public money for poor relief, was forced to borrow from leading townspeople to buy corn. Matters were bad again in 1639 when 25 of the jurats and members of the common council gave money or wheat for the use of the poor as well as putting an export duty on corn. Herrings, another staple food of the needy, were also in short supply in the town caused by the extensive commercial use of herring hangs followed by the export of the dried fish. The corporation decreed in 1610 that every person buying herrings to hang should sell or deliver 2,000 to the town's inhabitants at the same price that the fishermen would charge. Certain fines in the 17th century went directly to help the poor as well as confiscated meat and bread being sold illegally.

Ropewalk and Herring Hang in 1821

Vagrants and unlawful immigrants in the 17th century

The 1598 legislation allowed vagrants to be punished and sent to their own parish for help. Dover did not apply this strictly initially, sometimes giving relief rather than punishment, such as the woman likely to give birth who was given 3s. 4d. before being put out of town. From 1607, however, no relief was given; vagrants were seen as a moral and economic threat to the town, and, therefore, punished and sent away. Increasing numbers of vagrants and transient poor were taken from the streets and examined by magistrates. Many such were not really vagrants but intending immigrants to the town from other parts of the country.

The chronic poor were particularly vulnerable to poor harvests and economic downturns. Forced to move away to seek a living they were likely to become poorer and to travel further. During such crises the poor relief system was inadequate and local officials were keen to move these poor wretches on to avoid them becoming a charge on the poor rate. Coupled with fear of disorder caused by so many immigrants, the solution was to punish them.

Under the 1597 act, vagrants refusing to work were whipped and returned to the parish of their birth or of last settlement. Settlement was one year in one location. The definition of vagrant was vague giving parishes much scope! There were two types of vagrants: beggars who were rounded up by constables or even the mayor, whipped and sent away and, secondly, incomers recently arrived with enough money to lodge somewhere, albeit without permission, who were admonished and threatened. Sometimes these were bona fide travellers waiting overnight for a boat! Often they were allowed to stay for a few days, but if then they could not provide sureties to discharge the town of their expense or had not found a proper job, they had to leave or be punished as vagrants. The town clerk was paid for preparing banishment papers, lame rogues were carted out of town and porters escorted other offenders away. The beadle received 4d. for whipping a vagabond. Between 1604 and 1624 there were at least 234 true homeless vagrants and 54 incomers; between 1630 and 1640 there were 171 vagrants and 128 incomers. Numbers were lower during the months of harvest and December; February and March saw the highest numbers. Who were these vagrants? Not many were girls as they were easily put to domestic service. There were boys whose fathers had died, runaway apprentices, couples with and without children, women with children, men and women with spouses elsewhere, women on their own, wives whose husbands had left them or had left their husbands, widows with and without children.

By the 17th century incomers, those wishing to settle in the town from other parts of Kent and England, became a problem, particularly labourers who came to Dover to work but with no means to become freemen. In 1609 the corporation decided that too many were settling in the town and decreed that houses were not to be let to incomers unless they had certificates and sureties. The decree of 1609 deplored the many poor people who had settled in the town, living as man and wife, but unmarried. Couples suspected of not being married were examined. Half the cases presented to church courts in Dover between 1572 and 1640 were unmarried couples living together who presumably could not afford to marry. There were penalties for those letting accommodation to such people who had lived in the town for at least one year without permission of the mayor and jurats.

Only those with marriage certificates and sureties discharging the town of all poor relief responsibnilities were allowed. The biggest group of incomers were widows with as many as five children, all of whom were whipped and sent back to their place of birth, including two in their 60s. Unmarried couples were whipped and then the men were sent to their birth place whilst their female partners were held in prison for a few days before being sent away to ensure that the couple separated.

What problems poor newcomers to Dover had to face during this period 1500 to 1640! An artisan or tradesman wishing to establish himself in Dover needed impeccable sexual morality, enough money to get lodgings and friends in the town to provide sureties. Successful migration and resettlement was more difficult for the poor at the very time it was most necessary. The line between surviving as a poor craftsman and becoming a punished vagrant could be very narrow.

There was a distinct change in the care of the poor between 1500 and 1640 with a move away from personal to more impersonal systems of help. In the 16th century deserving inhabitants of the town, such as orphans, the temporarily disabled, temporarily impoverished men and women, would have been helped in a practical way by placing them in the care of families a little better off than themselves rather than institutionalising and then criminalising them, which was a feature of the various poor laws introduced.

Chapter 3

POOR LAWS AND THEIR IMPLEMENTATION 1535-1833

Help was given to the poor of the parish as well as to travellers in need by charities and local administrators. Small charitable endowments for the needy provided for only a handful of people, usually with parish officers as trustees or the corporation, in boroughs such as Dover. There were also parochial charities providing relief in kind – food (usually bread), fuel and clothing, but rarely money. This was only to specified poor such as widows, tradesmen who had fallen on hard times, aged men or poor seamen and then only once or a few times a year. More help was obviously needed.

Bequests to St. Mary's Church

Surviving records of bequests to St. Mary's go back to 1482. At this time it was usual for moneyed individuals upon their death to make bequests to a church in return for prayers said for their souls. The 1482 bequest by Thomas Fuller was to pay for a priest to say mass at St. Mary's and 6s. 8d. to repair the church forever! A combination of more poor with the population increase and traditional help from the monasteries and other religious institutions drying up, especially after the Dissolution of the monasteries by Henry VIII, meant that during the sixteenth century more bequests were intended to assist the needy of the parish. The first of these was in 1573 when Thomas Pepper left an income of 20 shillings a year for the relief of the poor of St. Mary's parish. Several bequests were for an annual distribution of bread. Nicholas Cullen's bequest of 1699 was to give every New Year's Day 13 shillings each to 20 poor widows who did not receive alms from the parish. By 1828 with increased income from properties, this was worth £5 a year to each widow. Help for poor widows was frequent. The well known Dover diarist, Thomas Pattenden, left stock providing sufficient income to maintain the fence around his grave in St. Mary's Churchyard with the remainder to help widows of seamen. Some

St. Mary's Church in 1814

bequests were never fully implemented and others were soon lost. This was often because bequests came from designated property of the deceased, but, without any provision for maintaining the property, it soon fell into decay and, if unoccupied, rental income ceased.

16th century poor laws

A series of parliamentary acts were designed to control beggars and vagabonds and to encourage local support for people in need. In 1535 the parish was made responsible for the impotent poor – those who had no choice. Private alms were forbidden, but the priest and churchwardens could collect charitable donations on Sundays. The Poor Law of 1563 called for 'two able-bodied persons or more to be appointed gatherers and collectors of the charitable alms of all the residue of people inhabiting in the parish.' Often those appointed were the chuchwardens and the act gave them limited powers to compel generosity as well as encouraging it! In 1572 magistrates were given authority to deal with those who refused to give alms. Licences for begging, introduced in 1530, were abandoned and a fine imposed for private alms giving, which could encourage begging. The office of Overseer of the Poor was also created, appointed by the Church Vestry and approved by Justices of the Peace. They supervised endowments and other charitable funds, collected any fines allocated to the relief of the needy and were used later to assess inhabitants for a poor rate. An act of 1597 allowed a poor rate with relief divided into 'indoor' for those maintained in poorhouses and 'outdoor' for those still in their own homes. The act also enabled the overseers to erect a poorhouse at the ratepayers' expense, to provide work for able paupers and, if possible, to apprentice pauper children. Provision was also made for the education of children in the workhouse, but this was usually observed in the breach.

1601 Poor Law

The spread of compulsory poor rates rather than alms in the 16th century culminated in the Poor Law of 1601 which became the foundation of relief until 1834. This included provision of work for the able-bodied.

Church vestry meetings were established responsible for levying a poor rate on occupiers of houses and land, which had to be confirmed by two Justices of the Peace who could not refuse or amend the rate. Public notice of the rate had to be given on the next Sunday after JPs had approved it by affixing it to the church doors before the service.

Churchwardens were appointed as overseers, up to four per parish, who had to be substantial householders nominated by JPs. Their duties were to levy and collect a poor rate to meet expenses, pay out as necessary, produce quarterly accounts, keep a rate book, a book of income and expenditure, a balance sheet for auditors each half year and a return of property. Only relief approved by the vestry or JPs could be given except in absolute necessity. The purpose was to relieve the sick and aged by providing food and lodging in poorhouses (indoor relief) or to provide outdoor relief for them in the form of cash, food, clothing and coal as well as finding work for the able-bodied poor in workhouses or houses of correction.

1662 Act of Settlement

A fundamental principle of the 1601 Poor Law was that each parish should be responsible for its own poor. Parishes were willing to help their own but were also eager to move on the needy who had come from other parishes. Disputes between parishes were frequently heard at Quarter Sessions. The 1662 Act of Settlement resolved this whole question. Those becoming a charge on the parish could be removed to their parish of legal settlement (i.e. of their birth), but if not removed within 40 days, a stranger could claim that he was settled and could become a charge on the poor rate.

Later Acts of 1685 and 1691 developed these provisions – claims on a parish could be based upon birth there, marriage to a parishioner, holding of a parish office or paying of a parish rate, bound by indenture as an apprentice to a parishioner, renting a house worth £10 a year or residence in the parish for 40 days without complaint. By the 1697 Act a poor person could enter any parish provided he brought from his parish of settlement a certificate that he would be received back if he became a charge. Removal orders were then made as necessary. Under this act paupers were obliged to wear a capital 'P' on their clothing and so attracted the nickname of 'badgers'. After 1699 the cost of transporting vagrants to the colonies fell on county funds not parishes, increasing the numbers of migrant workers and unemployed who took advantage of free travel and subsistence! A 1723 act allowed vagrants' children to be apprenticed against the will of the parents and bastard children did not receive a settlement certificate in the parish of their birth. Anybody sheltering a vagrant could be fined £2.

St. Mary's Poorhouse

The 1723 Workhouse Test Act authorised the building of workhouses and also allowed payments to persons who agreed to look after a poor person for a specified period. Otherwise the needy were obliged to enter a workhouse to obtain relief. As a consequence, in 1725 Mayor Charles Smith ordered that the corporation's old store house, standing on a low cliff on the west side of Limekiln Street in the Pier District be leased to St. Mary's Parish for conversion into a poorhouse. This large poorhouse was used until 1795. Statham in his history of Dover adds that in 1751 the corporation decided to sell the building used by St. Mary's to enable them to pay some debts, but this did not happen and it continued as a poorhouse. St. Mary's appointed a beadle in 1739 to help 'in taking up beggars and passing vagrants' and in 1769 two children illegally removed from Eastry workhouse to St. Mary's workhouse were promptly sent back!

In 1772 James and Joseph Willis were appointed Churchwardens, Henry Wood and William Walker Overseers for Town; William Coivley and Thomas King Overseers for the Pier. From St. Mary's Town and Pier Poor Book of 1776 we know that occupiers of lands, houses and buildings within the parish were levied 12d. in the pound for poor relief. Details of monies due and paid by everybody were recorded – Peter Fector, the banker, was a prominent payer – and a total of £289 6s. was collected. The frustration of St. Mary's vestry meeting was apparent when in 1786 it issued a warning to inhabitants 'who make it a common practice of unlawfully taking into their houses inmates and lodgers who do not belong to this parish but frequently become chargeable thereto'.

In 1792 a plan for a union of St. Mary's and St. James' parishes for poor relief purposes was approved by St. Mary's Parochial Church Council. It is recorded that 'St. Mary's parish workhouse and poor therein were in such a state that required amendment' and therefore called for a report. This stated that the 'Poor therein are much neglected and their morals greatly corrupted' and recommended the building of a new workhouse shared with St. James' parish. Their poorhouse was in Woolcomber Street, where the able bodied did wool combing. This proposal came to nothing.

By the 18th century a number of expedients other than the workhouse had crept into the system with variations in the administration of poor law around the country, such as the roundsman system where unemployed were sent from farm to farm to find farmers who would employ them for a meagre wage supplemented by the parish. There was also the labour rate, compelling each ratepayer to employ a certain number of labourers according to his poor rate assessment or to pay the parish an equal sum if there were no work. In 1795 with much poverty due to high prices and low wages, justices meeting at Speenhamland in Berkshire devised a system to supplement wages from the poor rate based upon the price of bread, which became law under Young's Act of 1796 and was known as the Speenhamland system. Child allowances to labourers in work for fourth and subsequent children was common. Outdoor relief was given in kind, particularly fuel, rent, rates, housing and subsidised food. However, the system encouraged employers to underpay in the knowledge that their workers would receive help from the parish and so the numbers applying for relief increased.

The authorities tried hard to prevent paupers from other parishes being a burden on their budgets. This was sometimes alleviated by income from bounties received from navy and military authorities for press-ganged men and from prosecutions following discovery of illegitimacy. It all helped to keep poorhouse costs down.

1782 Gilbert Act

The 1782 Gilbert Act 'For the Better Relief of the Poor' brought more changes, attempting in some respects to humanise the administration of workhouses. Independent inspectors were appointed, orphan children were to be boarded out elsewhere and children under seven were not separated from their parents. Paupers were not sent to workhouses more than 10 miles from their own parish and the requirement to wear a pauper's badge was abandoned, if the person was of good character. Workhouses were to be used for children, the aged and infirm, but not for the able-bodied. In many towns and villages the parish was too small a unit to be effective. Many could not afford to establish a workhouse and few

Elham Poorhouse and Master's House in 2006

able to manage one efficiently and so the Act allowed parishes to form unions to build and administer them. St. Mary's adopted the act but it did not reduce the rising poor rate.

The Gilbert Workhouse at Elham, an 18th century building, still stands in the High Street, although converted into an attractive private dwelling, and it is still called the Poor House with the master's house adjoining.

At a vestry meeting of St. Mary's in 1795 it was said that the existing poorhouse was in a wretched state, costing a lot but without making the tenants sufficiently comfortable and was totally unfit for its purpose. It was decided to build a new house in a better situation regulated by the new Gilbert Act. This was controversial because there was a proposal not to build a new

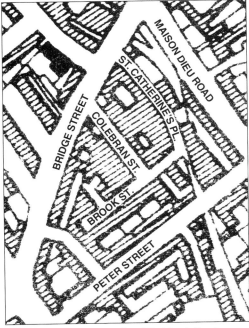

St. Catherine's Place - site of St. Mary's Poorhouse now part of Netto car park

workhouse since it was already proving difficult to collect the increasing poor rate. Nevertheless, ground was purchased in St. Catherine's Place, Charlton and built upon. Following completion in 1796 records state, 'Poor now well provided for … by the side of the river … a handsome appearance from the road.' Inmates were employed on its land between Peter Street and Bridge Street. The old house in the Pier District was sold for £1142 in 1798.

In 1806 land was purchased in front of the new workhouse 'to prevent nuisance and annoyance thereto' and in the same year a Collector of Poor Rate under Gilbert's Act was appointed at a salary of £20.

Lessening the pressure of the poor rate

A pamphlet published in 1819 by an anonymous parishioner of St. Mary's, entitled 'Lessening the pressure of the poor rate' provides some interesting suggestions for reducing costs for the rate payers of St. Mary's. At the time there were 90 men, 75 women, 50 boys and 46 girls in residence at St. Mary's poorhouse each costing on average 4 shillings a week to keep plus another £1200 a year relief for the outpoor. Financial benefits gained from the scavenging and spinning by residents totalled £235 a year, although parishioners paid for the scavenging anyway! It was suggested that much more gainful employment could be found for all the inmates capable of work: for men: tailoring, shoemaking, twine spinning, school slate making, patten making, mat and mop making and chair seats; for aged females, knitting; for the middle-aged, the making of poor quality clothes; for girls, shoe binding and for children, straw plaiting. Each of these new tasks would cost about £20 to introduce (teaching the task). Each child could earn 3 shillings a week and every other inmate could generate a similar amount, which would almost cover the cost of their keep. This would leave only the sick, the very infirm and the very young as a burden on the parish. It was also suggested that children could receive instruction to make them useful members of society. During the summer they could be taught to read before breakfast and then work and play for the rest of the day. In winter with daylight so much later, reading could be taught for one hour after the 8am breakfast followed by work until the midday meal, then play for one hour and work until dark! The anonymous writer also addressed the unacceptable £1200 cost of the outpoor which would keep 114 of them in the workhouse for a year. With 200 outpoor it would be cheaper to put them into the workhouse and make them work, making a saving of £1,000 a year. Most of these were not sick or infirm, but unemployed in distress and capable of work. The writer realised that the workhouse might not be able to house everybody and suggested that a hospital for the sick could be built from the savings! Whilst there is no evidence that these suggestions were adopted at the time, some of them were introduced nationally at a later date.

Sturgess Bourne Act

St. Mary's vestry learned that in 1827 there were seven lunatics in the workhouse, including two kept chained to their beds, one of whom had almost murdered another inmate. In 1828 it was agreed to exchange a piece of land belonging to

John Finnis with part of the workhouse garden. St. Mary's agreed to adopt the 1819 Poor Law Act in 1829. This was the Sturgess Bourne Act by which parishes were able to employ fulltime paid overseers and vestry decisions could be overturned by paupers appealing to magistrates who were often more generous! With increased pauperism vestries appointed standing committees to consider applications called 'select vestries'. In the same year it was decided that workhouse inmates of St. Mary's should make hop bags, sheeting etc. to provide useful employment and profit. The Master and Mistress were deemed competent to supervise the 'manufactory.' In 1832 the select vestry complained that the workhouse master allowed 15 ounces of meat to every inmate and that 164 gallons of strong beer were consumed during March. Frustration surfaced again in 1832 when St. Mary's refused to readopt the Gilbert Act, 'This Vestry is of the opinion that nothing whatsoever has been brought before them that would induce the parish to resort again to the administration of the Parish Affairs under the Gilbert Act.'

The end of St. Mary's Workhouse

Under the 1834 Poor Law Act ratepayers of the parish agreed to sell the workhouse and land and to use the money as the new Poor Law Commissioners decided – 1.5 acres of land in Charlton parish in the deeds of 1794 used as a workhouse and hospital for ease and reception of the poor of the parish plus a parcel of land dating from 1829. The Parish Meeting agreed that Churchwardens and Guardians should obtain permission from the Poor Law Commissioners to borrow the money arising from the sale of the workhouse and to lend the same to the new Guardians of Dover Union to help build a new 'hospital.' St. Mary's Charlton workhouse closed on 15 September 1837.

Many parishes paid passage money to Australia plus a clothing and provisions grant and money for land. For instance in July 1837 St. Mary's vestry agreed to advance £12 to Mrs. Welch to enable her and her family to emigrate to New Zealand which with the sale of her furniture would be enough. This facility was not generally available, however, for a later meeting refused to assist somebody else to emigrate.

Records of St. Mary's Workhouse

Many detailed records of the day to day running of St. Mary's workhouse survive in the Canterbury Cathedral Archives.

The admissions books record the names of those admitted, the date, by whom, the reason and when and why discharged. Reasons for admission include superannuated vagrant, sick, born a bastard, big with child, admitted with mother. There are lists of those living in – the inpoor – with comments, including 'mother married to a black', 'in with his mother,' 'parents dead,' 'father an American,' 'parents in the house.'

There are lists of those with settlement certificates, both those removed out of the parish and those removed in. In some years there were none or very few with more being removed in than being moved out – as an example, under surnames beginning with 'W' 60 people were moved in between 1698 and 1782 but only 12 moved out.

The Work Account Book for In Poor' for 1798 to 1801 shows that payment to inmates for work ranged from 3d. to 5s. The following expenses are taken from the Governor's Accounts 1785-1811: payment for a burial 6s. 4d., for carrying J Wood to graveyard 7s. 4d., part of Mr. Dovey's funeral expenses 12s.10d; porterage of cotton to Deal 6d.; payment for day's work in garden 2s.; bill for milk 5s. 6d.; parsnips and cabbage 6d.; bushel of onions 4s. 6d. In addition every item of expenditure was recorded each day in the Governor's Day Book e.g. in the 1795-1830 book: bushel of apples 5s., birch brooms 6s. 6d.; May Brett for wine 6s. 11d., beer for month 8s. 6d., extra trouble one day 2s. 6d., two soldiers paid for work in garden 7s.

Yet another account book was the List of Outpoor and Amounts Received. In the records covering 1793-1818, payments range from 1 to 2 shillings a week for orphans and widows etc. In 1793 there were about 80 people a month, including about 27 bastards at a total cost of £2 9s. 6d. a month. Examination of the Miscellaneous Costs book 1793-1803 reveal mainly baptism expenses e.g. May 1796 baptising a child 1s. 9d., paid a midwife for Burville child 7s. 6d., June 1796 for baptising Burville child 1s. 9d., May 1796, paid Geo. Thomas for 7 coffins £3 10s. 6d. The usual rate for burial fees in 1799 for an adult was 7s. 6d. but an infant of six months cost only 5s. 6d.; in 1803 burying a traveller cost 4s. 6d. Also recorded in August 1803 was the sudden death in the heat of Susanna Hopper aged 75.

The General Accounts book for 1804-1812 reveals that in 1804 provisions stock was £273 2s. 2d.; clothes and manufactory stock £120 15s. 3d.; paid for removals (people) for the year £60 13s.; births, funerals and burials for the year £12 5s. 6d. Total expenditure from April 1803 to March 1804 was £230 0s. 4d. with total receipts of £2372 10s. 8d. Expenditure on the poorhouse was £361 18s. In 1805 the income from the poor rate was £1237 4s. 6d. In 1806-7 receipts were £40 14s. 10d. less than expenditure. Some of the costs were: Outpoor £297 6s. 10d., removals and appeals £22 0s.1d, surgery, lawyers, bonds and interest £599 9s. 6d.

The Case Book for 1802-48 contains details of many difficult personal situations submitted for opinion or decision. The interesting case of Jane Weymouth in 1802 is a good example. She arrived in Dover with son George, aged eight months, from St. Peter's in Thanet, having been brought up in the workhouse of St. Peter the Apostle. At about 15 years of age she hired herself to John Wood of Sandwich as a servant, lived there for over a year and then had a bastard child, which was put out to be cared for at 1s. 6d. a week. To pay for it she hired herself as a wet nurse at 3s. 6d. a week to James Neale of St. Mary's Dover with the permission of the officers of St. Clement's Sandwich. After 11 months she carried on as a servant to Mr. Neale at £5 a year for another nine months. Following this, she hired herself to a Mr. Merrow, victualler, for five months and then Mr. Goodman for six months. Then she married George Weymouth, a mariner, born in Guernsey, who was put ashore and hospitalised at Portsmouth where she supposed he had died, not having heard from him. The question submitted for decision was, "Was Pauper Settlement in St. Clement's altered by hiring herself to Mr. Neale and having a child?" The answer was that as the hiring was not for a year it did not alter the settlement.

The Clothing Ledger listed clothing given to the poor such as coats, waistcoat, breeches, shoes, vests and shirts e.g. Richard Ratcliffe was given two pairs of shoes, a shirt and a hat. Women were given long gowns, short gowns, petticoats and shifts. The payment of men and women's pence money ranging from 3d. to 12d a week was recorded in the Inventories and Disbursements book.

The Governor's Work Book recorded sundry work done in the workhouse by inmates ranging from 3d. to £1 6s. per month and his Stock Book listed all the clothing and linen plus removals from stock with names, items and value e.g. gown at 1s. 6d., breeches 6d., shoes 4s. 6d. and a clock 6s. 6d. In house poor and out poor were shown separately.

The Weekly Account book of 1772-76 details work undertaken in the house as linen weaving, making jackets and eight washerwomen at 12d. a day. Boys 'beeling' and/or 'breeving' appear regularly.

There were Bill Books with details of banking and Monthly Account books. For a week in February 1833 there were sundry payments to Mr. Hiller, the Assistant Overseer: Outpoor £27 3s., Outparishes £5 18s., Bastards £2 7s. 5d., Stones 19s. 9d. In Mr. Hiller's payments book individual payments by him to the outpoor were recorded – money for rent, coals, transport from elsewhere and to casual poor.

Disbursements by the governor, Ebenezer Masters, for a three month period were recorded as: provisions £2 1s., pence money £15 11s. 7d., manufactory £2 9s., births 4s. 6d., furniture repairs £3 11s. 3d. and petty expenses 11s. 3d.

Payment of the poor rate and amounts due per property were recorded in the Rate Arrears account, which showed the address, whether poor people or not, empty properties and any arrears owed. The entry for June 1825 shows rates paid of £240 11s. 6d. and arrears of £83 4s. 6d.

The Guardians' Day Book listed the expenses of removing people, including the ultimate removal – the cost of funerals.

Meetings of St. Mary's vestry

The St. Mary's Vestry minutes of 1835-36 record grants made to people leaving the poorhouse of 10s., £1 1s. etc. Of more interest, the rations of inmates are given: butter 1 ounce per person 4 days weekly; cheese 1 1/2 ounces on 3 days; meat 9 ounces each meat dinner; pork 3 ounces each pork dinner; soap 3lbs. for every 10 persons weekly; bread 3/4lb. for each person daily; sugar 6lbs. weekly for the whole house.

At each meeting there was a report upon the numbers in the poor house, for instance 'In the house Men 71, Women 84, Boys 42, Girls 32 = 229 plus 3 babies. Decisions were made on the people to be admitted and goods to be purchased e.g. 1,218lbs. of bread, 5 barrels of malt beer, 4 1/2 barrels of strong beer; meat per person twice weekly, pork once; 53lbs. butter, 3lbs. candles, 66lbs. cheese, 2lbs. lump sugar, 13lbs. soap, 1 bushel of pears, 1 pound of tea, 1 pound of pepper, 1 gallon of vinegar, 1 pound of coffee, 3 sacks of potatoes and 4 1/2 gallons of porter. It can be seen that the Vestry Meeting exercised very tight control. At one meeting it approved a pair of shoes for somebody and the purchase of two dozen knives and forks for the children. They also wanted to know how much clothing had been issued over the previous two months and why!

Help from the town

After many years of war with France peace had come in 1815. Demobilisation plus prolonged depression increased the numbers of poor. Dover was burdened with wives and families left by regiments and by foreigners 'passed' down the country to return to the continent. A meeting of leading Dover townsmen concerned about the needy was held on 26 December 1816 with Revd. John Maule in the chair, which resolved to establish a society to relieve the poor 'with good meat soup during the winter season appears to be a most desirable object.' It also resolved to ask the Mayor to call a meeting of Dover and its vicinity inhabitants to carry this into effect. This subsequent meeting was held at the Town Hall on 31 December 1816 with Thomas Mantell, the Mayor, in the chair. It was agreed to form a Soup Society and to form a committee of 38 with powers to co-opt more which should meet on the first Monday of every month with a subcommittee of ten meeting once a week. Sixteen were to be appointed superintendents assisted by one paid person of which four were to attend daily to prepare and apportion ingredients for the boiler and enter in the proper book.

Dover Soup Society Notice 1816

Superintendents who did not attend would be fined three shillings. Good meat soup would be made twice a week from best quality meat and delivered on Tuesdays and Fridays at 11 am. Apparently eight quarts of soup could be made from every £1 subscribed. The poor would be charged 1d. a quart. The committee included Thomas Mantell, Revd. J. Maule, J. M. Fector, Samuel Latham, William Knocker, John Shipdem, Edward Rutley, J. W. Pilcher, W. R. Dickeson and W. Sankey.

Eighteen years later in 1834 the town adopted a ticket system entitling vagrants to bread and a night's lodging in the workhouse.

River Workhouse

The needs of the poor also had to be met in the parishes surrounding St. Mary's. As the numbers of needy increased, more money was required and administration of the Poor Law

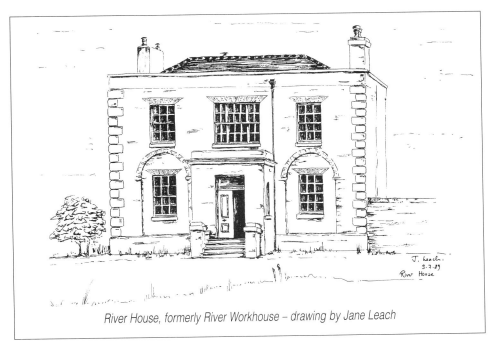

River House, formerly River Workhouse – drawing by Jane Leach

became difficult for unpaid part-time parish officers. Supervision by the parish church vestry meeting was often inadequate. The 1782 Gilbert Act had encouraged parishes to group together to make more efficient units to maintain workhouses and, consequently, the River Poor Law Union was formed on 14 March 1791, comprising the parishes of River, Whitfield, Buckland, Charlton, Hougham, Alkham and Capel Le Ferne. Folkestone and Walmer joined in 1792. By 1799 the Union covered 13 parishes including St. James' Dover, but not St. Mary's. The River Workhouse was built and opened in 1793. The main building and some outbuildings still survive as a private house in Valley Road, River. Work was provided about the workhouse for those able, about half the total, or away from the workhouse.

The numbers receiving relief between 1795 and 1802 were:

	Outdoor	Indoor
1795/6	113	127
1799/00	112	152
1800/01	154	111
1801/02	162	160

The completely destitute went into the workhouse. Help for those outside the workhouse was a shilling a week for the infirm and those with large families.

A report by Sir Francis Head, an Assistant Poor Law Commissioner, following a visit in 1832 stated, 'The River Workhouse is a splendid mansion. The dignity and elegance of its architecture, its broad double staircase, its spacious halls, the lofty bedrooms and its large windows form a delightful retreat, splendidly contrasted with the little ratepaying hovels at its feet.' Whether Sir Francis approved of the accommodation or thought it too comfortable for its purpose is not clear!

River Parish Church vestry minutes reveal that on 21 June 1835 the meeting heard a complaint about James Jenny, an inmate, about his dinner, which comprised part of a pig's foot, a pig's tail, a small piece of pork and smaller pieces of mutton when mutton only was ordered; the governor was asked to explain why the order was not fulfilled particularly as the governor had forfeited the confidence of the vestry in so many other instances. The meeting was of the opinion that he should no longer be entrusted with the concerns of the workhouse!

The 1834 Poor Law led to the formation of a new union, expanding the River Union and later including St. Mary's parish.

Chapter 4

POOR LAW AMENDMENT ACT, 1834
AND LATER CHANGES

Introduction

The old Poor Law system had started to break down by 1815. The Napoleonic wars, bad harvests, the introduction of farm machinery and population increase added to the problem. The cost of poor relief soared between 1784 and 1832 by which time it was estimated to be more than £8 million in the country as a whole. It had become increasingly difficult to collect the poor rate and parishes could barely cope. By 1830 the country was in a state of unrest and the Swing Riots in the south raised fears of revolution. Something had to be done; reform was necessary. An 1832 commission of enquiry into the poor law concluded that if paupers were made miserable, they would decline in number. The resulting Poor Law Act of 1834 was a return to the spirit of the Elizabethan Poor Law and aimed to set the poor to work. *The Daily Telegraph* commented that the Act 'will prove as great a curse, as hideous a monster, as ever inflicted on the country.'

Causes of extreme poverty

There were conflicting theories about the causes of extreme poverty. Whilst inventions such as the threshing machine deprived agricultural labourers of winter work, the rising population, caused by improved medical practices, meant that people were living longer. Couples were also marrying younger, providing more opportunities for childbirth. William Cobbett in his book, Rural Rides, commented upon 'the beggarly houses and the ragged, dirty, poor people of East Kent. Some people were convinced that the poor were responsible for their own poverty and that the old Poor Law encouraged population growth by enabling a poor man to marry, even though there was little prospect of him supporting a family, because he could rely upon parish assistance. A widely held belief amongst the better off was that the poor should accept their lot in life. This lack of compassion included some at least of the clergy. The Revd. H. Milman wrote in 1832 that 'the workhouse should be a place of hardship, of coarse fare, of degradation and humility; it should be administered with strictness and with severity; it should be as repulsive as is consistent with humanity.'

The 1834 Act

The 1834 Act was radical, sweeping away the old poor law to meet the economic and social changes. There was a new administrative framework and a new approach to relief of poverty. Independent parish control of relief was discarded in favour of local Boards of Guardians responsible to a central body, the Poor Law Commission. Some parishes had already grouped themselves together voluntarily to support the expense of a workhouse, but the act made this compulsory with the aim of combining 13,000 parishes nationwide into 573 unions by 1838, which was not in fact achieved until 1868. The practice of outdoor relief was abandoned and able-bodied men had to seek relief in the workhouse or not at all. Relief was to be concentrated in large workhouses where conditions should be 'less eligible' than those of the worst paid independent labourer, thereby acting as a self test for the applicant – will I be worse or better off in the workhouse? Only the truly destitute would seek admission and the idle would be deterred. This would lead to self reliance in the labouring classes as well as a substantial reduction in poor rates! However, ratepayers did not really benefit if the cost of new workhouses are taken into account.

The act substantially reduced indoor relief for the able-bodied initially but it increased again later. Despite its aim, the act curtailed but did not eradicate outdoor relief. Guardians soon found loopholes in the law enabling them to give outdoor relief and the vast majority of (able bodied) paupers managed to live outside the workhouse with doles in cash or kind from guardians. Increasingly, workhouses contained the old, the young, the sick and the mentally ill.

Boards of Guardians

One or more guardians to administer these unions were elected from each parish or town in the union for one year by open ballot of ratepayers and property owners with a minimum property qualification of £40 rateable value. Only those poor rated and paid up could vote with up to six votes according to the rateable value of their property. Justices of the Peace were ex officio guardians. Whilst subject to the Poor Law Commission, in practice the guardians enjoyed considerable autonomy. Women were entitled to become guardians if they possessed the necessary property qualifications, but in practice the first was not elected until 1875.

Guardians met weekly or fortnightly to consider all applications for relief and decided the amount and nature of any assistance. They received reports on the state of the workhouse, examined the accounts and gave necessary directions on management and discipline. All purchases and contracts for the supply of furniture, food and clothing and maintenance of the workhouse were authorised by them. They also had power to bury any poor person and charge the expense to the appropriate parish if within the union area or where they had died or where the body was. The burial costs of tramps dying in the union were met from union funds. Guardians could recover from the belongings of paupers the costs expended on them either during their lives or upon their death but had no powers to find inmates outside work or to help prevent destitution.

The powers of JPs to order relief were restricted to sudden and urgent temporary assistance plus any two JPs could order outdoor relief for anybody, from personal knowledge of a JP, or unable to work through old age or infirmity without residing in the workhouse. JPs and clergy could visit the workhouse at any time to examine food, clothing, bedding and the condition of inmates and could report anything amiss to the next Quarter Sessions court. Urgent matters such as contagious disease could be dealt with immediately by applying to other JPs for immediate action. There were also regular visits from Poor Law inspectors from the Commission and Guardians appointed visiting committees to examine the workhouse once a week.

Officers

With the consent of the Poor Law Commissioners, Guardians had power to appoint paid officials of at least 21 years of age, but nobody convicted of felony, fraud or forgery. These were: the clerk to the Guardians, treasurer, chaplain, medical officer, master and matron, schoolteacher, porter, nurse, relieving officer, superintendent of outdoor labour plus any assistants. The master and matron had to be able to keep accounts, the relieving officer had to be fulltime and have no other work, the nurse (from 1847) had to be able to read directions on medicines, the medical officer had to be qualified in both medicine and surgery and the chaplain was subject to the consent of the bishop. In the early years the master, often a former policeman or NCO, was seen as little more than a jailer – punishment rather than rehabilitation being the obvious intention. Salaries were low with no right to pension until 1896, duties were tiresome and the master was tied to the workhouse as much as the inmates! In 1880 a master with 500 inmates enjoyed a salary of £80 compared with a prison governor's salary of £600. The matron was usually the master's wife. Medical officers, supplementing earnings from private practice, had to provide their own drugs and medicines at first. Any nurses were often female inmates who were given a reward for laying out the dead, but trained nurses appeared in greater numbers after 1850. Workhouse staff ate the same meals as inmates but 'enjoyed' larger portions!

Buildings

A priority for every union was to build a new, large workhouse or enlarge and adapt an existing poorhouse, but cost was restricted to no more than 10% of the annual poor rate, although unions were allowed to borrow the money if necessary. The Poor Law Commissioners' report of 1835 included model plans for new workhouses and local plans had to be approved by them. Only 6 foot headroom was allowed in living quarters as 'well built, substantial rooms bring a luxury attractive to the pauper.' Old parish poorhouses had been little more than domestic dwellings, like the building that survives at Elham, compared with the new workhouses for 500 inmates. Once a year all rooms had to be limewashed. All furniture had to be kept in good repair and buildings well maintained, including heating and ventilation. Needless to say the least used room was the most ostentatious – the boardroom where the Guardians met.

Relief

Relief for the able-bodied and their families had to be in the workhouse except for sudden and urgent need, sickness or accident, expenses of burying a member of the family, a widow for the first six months, a widow with legitimate, dependent offspring (and no bastards born after widowhood). Wives of husbands

Casual Ward of Marylebone Workhouse, London – drawing by Sue Boulden

'beyond the seas,' in custody or in a lunatic asylum were treated as widows for relief purposes.

Any assistance given to the old, the lame, the blind, the impotent or those unable to work could be recovered by order of two JPs from parents, grandparents or children if they were able to pay, but no relief given to the able-bodied could be recovered. Any husband, father or mother deserting a family and leaving them as a charge on the poor rate could be punished as rogues and any goods seized by order of two JPs. Mothers had to maintain any illegitimate children until they were 16, if they stayed unmarried or widowed – assisted by the father if an affiliation order existed. Marriage relieved the biological father of any responsibility and a man marrying such a woman took on the responsibility until illegitimate children reached 16 or until the death of the mother.

The poor could be helped to emigrate, but not more than £10 each could be paid except for orphans or deserted children where the full cost could be met, provided such children gave their consent before a magistrate.

The cost of keeping needy people in asylums also fell on the union. Guardians could pay the costs of keeping any blind, deaf and dumb paupers in institutions and could pay the costs of any such children's schooling.

Unions were also obliged to help any casual poor requiring immediate help, but could not remove them and could not recover the costs from the settlement parish.

Conditions of admission

Admittance to the workhouse was by signed order of the board of guardians, the relieving officer or the overseer. In urgent cases the master or matron could admit without an order. On admission new inmates went to receiving wards where they were thoroughly cleansed and medically examined before putting on the union uniform. For women this was a shapeless waist-less dress reaching to the ankles plus under-draws, a shift, long stockings and a poke bonnet; men wore shirts and ill-fitting trousers tied at the knee with thick vests, woollen draws and socks, a neckerchief and in cold weather a coarse jacket. Children's outfits made their life, particularly for the girls, a misery. Besides being a badge of pauperism, girls wore long woollen dresses all year round and hobnailed boots with iron tips. Their own clothes were removed, cleaned and stored ready for their eventual, possible discharge. Porters could search for banned items such as alcohol, cards, dice, matches and improper printed material. There was nowhere to keep personal possessions other than in or under the bed. Men were not permitted razors and sometimes were only allowed to shave once a week. All had hair cut in the same rough and ready manner; boys' and girls' hair was cropped.

Casuals, i.e. tramps, had to be admitted. They were then given a bowl of gruel and a bed in an unheated casual ward. Next morning they were set to work oakum picking, wood chopping, stone breaking or digging the vegetable plot and could not leave before 11am nor, after 1871, before completing the work allocated.

The punitive approach was exercised through the physical conditions, the strict regime, diet, discipline and the monotony of the daily routine. Inmates lost their dignity, but also lost the right to vote, if they had it, which was not restored until 1918. Despite the harshness, Guardians did sometimes display compassion to the old, the sick and to children.

Husbands were separated from their wives, children from their parents. There were separate wards as far as possible: men infirm through old age or other causes, able-bodied men aged 15 and over, boys aged 7 to 15, infirm women, able-bodied women aged 15 and over, girls aged 7 to 15, children under 7. Even further segregation was possible according to morals and behaviour – 'unchaste women' were isolated from others, if possible, with even fewer privileges; after all, poverty was their own fault due to their moral failing. Compassion did creep in – there was no need to separate infirm married couples provided separate sleeping compartments were provided.

The habit of work, albeit without pay, was instilled to encourage paupers to leave to find work. All were employed according to ability, but there was no work on Sundays, Christmas Day or Good Friday. Although Christmas Day was a day of rest, no festivities were allowed originally even if financed by local benefactors, but by 1847 Guardians were allowed to provide extras out of the poor rate.

The aged and infirm looked after children. Women cooked and washed clothes. Some received extra food or tobacco for their efforts. The skills of some inmates, such as painting and decorating, saved Guardians' money, but otherwise the work was tedious – stone breaking, firewood chopping, oakum picking.

Prayers were said before breakfast and dinner daily and worship every Sunday in the workhouse was compulsory – everybody attended except the sick, those of unsound mind, young children, those too infirm, or dissenters.

Any pauper could quit with his family after giving reasonable notice unless the Guardians directed otherwise.

Diet

Diets were strict and monotonous, mainly cheese, gruel, soup, potatoes and occasionally meat and bacon except on Christmas Day or by order of the medical officer. Quantities, which ranged from 137 to 182 ounces a week per person, were about half that allowed for prisoners. If any inmate asked the master to weigh the allowance of food at any meal, it had to be done and in the presence of the complainant and two others. Gradually, however, diets improved.

This diet, although monotonous and frugal, did provide three meals a day and was probably more than the average labourer ate. For such a labourer and his family, meat was a luxury they could seldom afford, but for most lack of a good meal and no sheets or blankets was still preferable to life in the workhouse. Nevertheless, during a labourer's lifetime, it was likely that he and his family would spend some time in the workhouse due to unemployment, sickness or old age.

Punishment

For serious disobedience the master could take an inmate to a magistrate who could punish by fine or imprisonment. Punishment within the workhouse involved restricted diet or confinement by order of the guardians. The master could also confine a person for 12 hours in aggravated circumstances. Corporal punishment by the master or teacher was only permitted for boys under 14. Bringing spirits into the workhouse without permission was punished by fine or imprisonment. Paupers absconding also went to prison!

Children

The Act provided for the setting up of schools inside the workhouses for child inmates and was, therefore, a forerunner of state-provided education later in the century. The education of children was taken more seriously inside the workhouse than outside, possibly because it might help to break the cycle of destitution. A child with some education would have a better chance of employment if taught a trade and if he was able to read and write. More important perhaps, such a child would not be a burden on the rates as an adult! There was, in theory if not always in practice, three hours schooling daily in reading, writing, arithmetic and Christian religion plus instruction to fit them for 'service, usefulness, industry and virtue'. In the first few years after 1834 some of those employed as school masters and mistresses were barely educated themselves. The workhouse teacher had a lowly status and had to supervise children outside school hours and could not leave the workhouse without the master's permission. Later in the 19th century there was a trend toward teaching outside the workhouse in normal day schools as well as a tendency to foster or adopt workhouse children. It also became increasingly common for children to be placed in separate children's homes. Between 1834 and 1908 one third of all receiving poor relief were under 16 years of age and until 1900 25% of workhouse inmates were children.

Apprenticeships

Poor boys often fared better than girls in preparation for a working life for they were often taught useful trades like shoemaking, tailoring and carpentry. The Poor Law Commissioners also encouraged the sending of boys into the Royal Navy, the Merchant Navy and the Army. Boards of Guardians were allowed to apprentice pauper children to tradesmen, but from 1847 no child under 9 years of age and no child unable to read or write his name could be apprenticed. Consent of the father was necessary if the child was under 16 (or mother if he had no father) and the consent of the child itself if he was himself over 14 years old. If he was under 14, the child had to be medically fit and no child could be apprenticed more than 30 miles away. The situation was discussed at a meeting of the Board with the child present (and a parent if under 16). After hearing any objections, the indenture was executed. Any such apprentices received an official visit twice a year and their condition was reported to the Guardians. These regulations regarding apprenticeships were one of the few situations where a pauper boy, living in the workhouse or outside it, was treated in the same way as a 'normal' boy.

On the other hand, girls were trained for a life of drudgery. From the age of nine they spent alternate days in the classroom and the needlework room. At 11

Workhouse boys picking oakum
– drawing by Sue Boulden

Wood chopping at Pontefract workhouse – drawing by Sue Boulden

their chores were extended to making all the workhouse beds, cleaning the dormitories and waiting upon the sick in the infirmary. At 14 a ten hour day was worked in the laundry or kitchen, cleaning staff quarters and waiting on table. This seems harsh to us in the 21st century, but working such long hours was normal for 19th century children on farms, in factories and the workhouse. Following this training, workhouse girls were ready to enter service – many as the only servant in the house working 16 hours a day for a few pounds a year. Consequently, many left for other work or returned to the workhouse as paupers.

Later changes

Workhouse beds were wooden originally, but by 1836 were made of iron. Men slept in single beds, but women in double beds – two to a bed – whilst children under seven slept three to a bed. The Poor Law Board Act of 1847 required Guardians to provide any married couple over 60 years of age with a separate bedroom if requested. By 1900, however, only 200 married couples enjoyed their own room in England and Wales.

During the century workhouse populations altered. The provision of outdoor relief to the able-bodied from mid century meant a smaller proportion of them in the workhouse – despite the original principle. After 1850 workhouses catered mainly for the old, sick, handicapped, children, unmarried mothers and vagrants with some relaxation of the regime for the old and handicapped. There was a substantial improvement in the treatment of the sick for conditions in sick wards attracted criticism from professionals and the Workhouse Visiting Society. Some new infirmaries were built as a consequence.

From 1856 any able-bodied person receiving relief could also receive assistance to provide schooling for any children aged 4 to 16 at a school approved by the Guardians. Assistance included maintenance, clothing and education, provided it did not exceed the cost of keeping the child in the workhouse.

Settlement and removal rules changed dramatically in 1865. Poor people were entitled to relief in their parish of settlement. Everybody was entitled to settlement where he or she was born until another later settlement was proved, since a later settlement superseded an earlier one. Settlement was acquired by birth, parentage, marriage (whereby a wife obtained the husband's settlement), apprenticeship, by renting a dwelling for a year, by payment of rates or by estate. Two magistrates could authorise removal to the latest place of settlement to receive assistance, but from 1865 residence of one year in a parish gave the right to irremovability; so few became chargeable in the first year that removals became rare. Receiving parishes had 21 days to object via the Quarter Sessions courts.

Under the Vaccination Acts of 1867 and 1871 all residents had to be vaccinated as a precaution against smallpox.

From 1868 the religious creed of all inmates was recorded and became open to inspection by any minister of religion who could visit to instruct the inmates, unless, if over 14, the person objected. Inmates were allowed out of the workhouse to attend a service of their own denomination if none was held in the workhouse. Children could not be compelled to attend a service other than that recorded, unless, if they were over 12, they wished to receive instruction in another creed.

The Poor Law Commission was succeeded in 1870 by the Local Government Board whose inspectors had powers to institute inquiries into the administration

Tramps waiting for admission – drawing by Sue Boulden

37

Dining at a large workhouse – drawing by Sue Boulden

of the poor law and attended, as observers, all Guardians' meetings in their area and every parochial meeting held for poor relief purposes.

The composition of boards changed with the extension of the electoral franchise. Elections of Guardians were held at the same time as parliamentary elections from 1894 and the property qualification was abolished. This led to more working class and female Guardians. Reports of Guardians' meetings in the local press made them more accountable and the whole system more transparent.

Towards the end of the 19th century attitudes to poverty began to change. It was no longer considered a crime to be poor but, although a more benevolent approach developed, the stigma of the workhouse remained.

20th century innovations

By the end of the 19th century many local friendly societies had sprung up with more than four million families contributing a quarterly fee of anything from three to ten shillings in return for the breadwinner receiving sickness benefit when ill. This was a safety net for those in work, but not for others. In London alone in 1905 77,000 people were in workhouses and 49,000 others were dependent upon poor relief handouts out of a population of 4.5 million.

The 1905 Royal Commission on Poor Law was unable to agree and a minority report recommended, however, abolition, but nothing happened.

The introduction of state old age pensions in 1908 and state sickness and unemployment insurance in 1911 heralded a new national approach to the problem of poverty. Legislation provided non-contributory pensions of 5s. a week for people over 70 or 7s. 6d for married couples, but only if annual income was less than £21 a year. Criminals and lunatics were not entitled. Despite its limited coverage, this Old Age Pensions Act represented a new and important use of taxation for the redistribution of income, constituting a move away from the hold of the poor law toward the development of the Welfare State.

Workhouses were renamed Poor Law institutions in 1913 and in 1918 electoral reform gave the vote to those on poor relief. The period after the First World War brought not a country 'fit for heroes to live in' but mass unemployment. Some Guardians distributed outdoor relief too liberally for the government's liking and in 1926 Neville Chamberlain as Conservative Minister of Health took direct control of poor relief when Guardians were thought to be too liberal – the Board of Guardians Default Act also enabled the government to restrict relief to striking miners' families. Between 1918-39 unemployment benefit was one third of the average wage.

The 1929 Local Government Act took effect in 1930 and entitlement to relief became means tested. Only the aged and infirm could apply for workhouse care but outdoor relief could be given if necessary. Local councils were to care for orphans. Local Boards of Guardians were dissolved and their powers were transferred to the county councils. Poor Law institutions were renamed Public Assistance institutions, but most remained with the same functions and inmates until 1945. The one minor change in the interim was that from 1938 aged inmates were given two shillings a week pocket money.

The post Second World War Labour government brought with it a definite change of policy and the introduction of the Welfare State. The 1948 National Assistance Act finally brought poor law to an end. Many workhouses were then demolished or converted into hospitals or old people's homes. Whilst nobody can regret the passing of this harsh regime, it did, however, save thousands of men, women and children from starvation. Many of the children received an elementary education and were taught a trade, opening the door to a better way of life.

Chapter 5

DOVER UNION AND WORKHOUSE

Rosemary Piddock's 1987 thesis for the University of Kent, entitled *Dover – a general assessment of its economic status in 1835*, paints a picture of Dover's economy upon which the 1834 Poor Law Amendment Act was imposed. The conclusion of the 1835 Report of the Royal Commission on Municipal Corporations upon Dover was that, whilst there was some poverty, the town was thriving. The corporation promoted trade by the acceptance of new freemen, licensing porters and allowing markets and trade to expand. As the 19th century progressed new employment opportunities provided by the holiday trade and paper manufacture offset job losses from the decline in the corn milling industry and the change from sail to steam in shipping services. The diversity of the town's trades and services encouraged employment. In addition to the traditional cross Channel industry, Dover had become a seaside holiday town and this, coupled with the substantial military establishments, created additional demands for goods and services. This satisfactory state of affairs was reflected in the population increase. In 1801 the parishes of St. Mary's and St. James' had a total of 7,084 living in 1708 houses. By 1831 it had risen to 11,922 living in 2,095 houses and by 1851, 15,076 people.

An Assistant Poor Law Commissioner, Sir Francis Head, a former army major, was charged with implementing the new 1834 Poor Law in Kent. Unlike the *Kent Herald*, which considered the Poor Law Act 'an attempt to drive the poor from misery to starvation,' Sir Francis believed in the new system stating, 'our wretched system of late Poor Laws has deprived the labourer and almost ruined the farmer.' He aimed to create 27 unions in Kent within a year despite opposition from some towns and villages. All unions had to agree maximum scales for outdoor relief and a uniform diet for new workhouses.

The new River Union

In February 1835 there was a meeting at the River Union workhouse chaired by Edward Rice MP and attended by Sir Francis Head and officers from the various parishes in the union plus representatives from St. Mary's Parish to discuss a proposal to dissolve the River Union and to form two larger unions based upon River and Eastry with a workhouse at both, but demolishing the poorhouse at Martin. The new River Poor Law Union was formed covering Alkham, Buckland, Capel, Charlton, Coldred, Denton, Dover Castle Liberties, East Cliffe, East Langdon, Ewell, Guston, Hougham, Lydden, Martin, Oxney, Poulton, Ringwould, River, St. James' Dover, St. Margaret's at Cliffe, Sibertswold, West Cliffe, West Langdon, Whitfield and Wootton. St. Mary's Dover joined in 1837 when inmates of St. Mary's outnumbered those in the rest of the new Union.

The first meeting of the Guardians of the new River Union was held at River on 1 May 1835. Sir Francis Head was present with 19 Guardians representing most of the parishes involved. Sir Francis addressed the meeting stating, '... the welfare of the labouring poor will depend upon your future proceedings ... a

Board of Guardians under the Poor Law Amendment Bill who will have at their disposal all the monies levied within the Union for the support and maintenance of the poor'. Henry Gilbert of Sibertswold was elected Chairman and Mark Sandford of Oxney, Vice Chairman. The Chairman resigned in April 1836 and was succeeded by Revd. J. Monins and Robert Potter became his Vice Chairman. William Croft was appointed clerk at £30 a year. Weekly meetings on Saturday morning at River Workhouse were agreed. The Union was divided into two districts with two Relieving Officers at £80 a year each and Latham & Co, local bankers, were asked to act as treasurer to the Union free of charge. It was also agreed to advertise for a medical gentleman to furnish medicines and attendance of every sort on the poor of the Union at £130 a year for the whole Union or £70 a year for certain parishes only and £25 for certain others. Larger workhouse accommodation was to be provided as soon as land was available and a building committee was appointed to seek a suitable site.

The minute book of the new Board of Guardians reveals that it had plenty to do in addition to planning the new workhouse. Caring for the poor continued both inside and outside the existing poorhouses and arrangements for the new system had to be made with the guidance of Sir Francis Head.

James Worsfold was appointed auditor. Newspaper advertisements were placed for tenders to supply 'middlings' i.e. coarse ground wheat as well as bread loaves made from best middlings. Samples of the middlings were to be delivered with the tenders! Those accepted were for: best middlings at £2 0s.10d. per 28lbs., bread at 1¼d. per pound and flour at 28 shillings per 5 bushels.

The Board of Guardians took over control of all outdoor relief from 6 June 1835. George Rutley, appointed Surveyor at £130 a year, was also appointed Medical Officer from 6 June at a salary of £60 a year but excluding midwifery and hernia trusses. For attending paupers outside the workhouse the fee was 4s. 6d. a case, excluding midwifery and trusses again! However, his total remuneration was capped at £130 a year. In December 1836 his basic salary was increased to £100 a year to take account of St. Mary's joining the union. This was increased again in May 1837 to £200 a year plus a fee of 15 shillings for each midwifery case, which was later reduced by the Poor Law Commissioners to 10 shillings a case. He supplied his own trusses! At the June 1835 meeting it was decided that relief for the able-bodied poor should be the same for all parishes in the union i.e. for a single man 10d. per day, for a couple one shilling plus 1d. for each child, but not exceeding 1s. 6d. in total for children! Half of the amount was to be in kind.

A letter received from Sir Francis Head on 13 June stated firmly, '… until you possess the power of establishing the difference between the conduct of the industrious labourer and the pauper you are without the means of creating that distinction which can alone enable you to resolve our society to a healthy state.'

The Guardians also resolved that relieving officers should not pay any relief to the able-bodied or to widows, not being aged or infirm, unless they produced a certificate from the parish overseer stating the number of days out of work and that 'due diligence in endeavour to obtain employment had been used and had not refused work offered.'

At another meeting in June it was resolved that an allowance should be made to illegitimate children beyond the amount actually paid by the reported father. Another decision was that the Governor should procure a decent suit and a pair of shoes for the boy, George Brett, going from the workhouse into service. As usual at these weekly meetings new applications for relief were considered. The Governor was authorised to renew contracts for provisions and, therefore, in July 1835 tenders were invited to provide: malt, barley meal, middlings, breasts of mutton, candles, butter, cheese, tea, salt, soap, sugar, pepper and coal and notice was given to the parishes of Wootton, Denton and Guston to pay their poor rate dues forthwith. It was also reported that the medical officer had provided trusses to such paupers that required them!

An important meeting of Chairmen and Vice Chairmen of all East Kent unions was held at Canterbury on 31 July where Sir Francis Head stated that fixed scales of relief were hostile to the principle of the 1834 Poor Law Act. Guardians must take into account for each person their previous earnings, time unemployed, reason for losing last employment, opportunities for reemployment since, character and conduct, so that a pauper should never be able to calculate the relief to be awarded. Because of its 'incomprehensible fluctuation' any pauper would learn that 'he could not safely rely on anything but his own industry.' However, Sir Francis did agree that if the 11 unions of East Kent wished to act uniformly, they could set a maximum for outdoor relief and diet for the workhouse. After several hours' discussion, it was agreed that relief should not exceed for a man, wife and six children 10 shillings and for a couple 5 shillings. The agreed diet for an able-bodied couple was: breakfast and supper – bread and cheese or butter (6 ounces of bread for a man, 5 for a woman with 1 ounce of cheese or half an ounce of butter); dinner – suet pudding and vegetables two days a week (1 pound for men and 10 ounces for women), one day meat pudding and vegetables (1 pound for men and 10 ounces for women) and bread and cheese for four days a week (7 ounces of bread and 1 ounce of cheese). The aged were to receive the same plus 1 ounce of tea with milk for breakfast and supper. Children would have bread and milk for breakfast and supper plus a proportion of the dinner diet as appropriate for their ages. The Medical Officer was to decide what the sick should have. The meeting also decided that one combined order for bedsteads should be made. The River Union agreed to adopt the Canterbury agreements.

Sir Francis Head interfered in matters small as well as great. He made recommendations to the Board that beds for male paupers in wards containing eight should have two berths in each corner and enclosed a drawing with his letter, showing how they should be fixed!

By August 1835 Sir Francis wanted some changes to the agreed diets, substituting gruel for children's breakfast and supper whenever it was inconvenient to provide milk. He also made a concession for the elderly – an additional meat pudding dinner a week for such of the very able old people whom the Guardians thought required it. However, he was not going soft because he commented on the generosity of the outdoor relief and the agreed maximum should not be exceeded, since it was above the wages of peasants anywhere in Europe and greater than the regular wages of many labourers in Great Britain and equal to Kent labourers' wages. There was a need to ensure that Guardians did not elevate paupers above the industrial labourer.

In September it was decided that bread would be baked in house in future, including bread distributed to various parishes and in October it was agreed that the Medical Officer could charge a shilling a day for paupers in the workhouse who did not reside within the Union area. During the same month the poor rate for the participating parishes were listed:

River	£1300	Ewell	£692	Oxney	£36
Denton	£373	Poulton	£150	E. Langdon	£396
Coldred	£569	Hougham	£1983	Sibertswold	£594
Wootton	£154	Lydden	£450	Alkham	£1189
West Cliffe	£303	Charlton	£875	W. Langdon	£29
Ringwould	£1115	Whitfield	£811	St. James	£3238
St. Margarets	£940	Buckland	£2251	Guston	£427
Capel	£555				

Total £18,450

A letter from Sir Francis Head in October extolled the benefits of ordering all bastards into workhouses. When Sir Francis moved on to organise West Kent he thanked all the boards for their support, "Guardians are non paid and are subject to prejudice, clamour and even violence but you will earn gratitude and respect."

John Bentley and his wife Susan were appointed governor and matron of the new workhouse at a combined salary of £90 a year to board his family and to furnish his apartments. They were also allowed coals and candles. The clerk's salary was increased to £80 a year. Revd. James Peto was appointed chaplain, but he resigned in 1836 and Revd. P. Lancaster from Barfrestone replaced him, but only until 1837 when Revd. E. Boys took over.

Some idea of the size of the workhouse can be gained from an advertisement placed in the local newspapers for 172 bedsteads and in February 1836 an order was placed for coffins 'planed, pitched and oiled' made of 3/4 inch board at the following prices: 7 foot long 10s. 10d., 6 foot 9s. 10d., 5 foot 8s. 10d., 4 foot 6s. 4d. and 3 foot 4s. 2d. Burial fees for paupers were set at a shilling each for the minister and for the clerk but 2s. 6d. for the sexton. This arrangement enjoyed a short life, since a meeting of unions at Canterbury adopted a resolution recommending no burial fees in future except for the sexton. It was also agreed at the same time that meat puddings were to be made of 3½lbs. crust with potatoes but no suet and 2½lbs. of boneless beef.

The new Assistant Commissioner attended a meeting of Guardians in February 1836 and agreed that the Poor Law Commission would not require unions to adopt uniform clothing for inmates.

Inclusion of St. Mary's Parish in the Union

In the following month he sent a letter proposing the admission of St. Mary's Parish to River Union. He attended a Guardians' meeting again during that month to try to persuade the Board to accept St. Mary's Parish, which would double the number of inmates of the workhouse. The Board was concerned about the increased cost, nevertheless, in July 1836 the Guardians submitted a request to the Poor Law Commission for St. Mary's Parish to join the River Union, which was approved. St. Mary's was to provide two Guardians and to contribute appropriately toward the expenses.

There was some friction when in August 1836 the Governor of St. Mary's Workhouse lined up his children on the bank opposite River Workhouse where they sang! The Board thought that this was disrespectful and complained to St. Mary's Vestry, but St. Mary's Governor explained that he had taken them to River to sing in order 'to remove that dread which had been erroneously instilled into their minds by many individuals in the Town of Dover.'

It was in April 1837 that the Board decided that as the greatest part of the population of the Union, which now included St. Mary's Parish as well as St. James', was in the Borough of Dover, the name should be changed to the Dover Union. By 13 July 1837 all the inmates of St. Mary's Workhouse had been moved to the new premises.

The new building

Only one week after the first meeting of the Guardians in May 1835 the building sub committee had reported that land belonging to the workhouse at River was the most suitable site for the new building. The Guardians decided to take legal advice as to whether they could erect buildings at River 'without the concurrence of the parish of River.'

Plans for the new workhouse were quickly accepted by Sir Francis and it was agreed to purchase land, but not to exceed £500, and to build a workhouse for no more than £3,000. The money was to be borrowed; the amount was less than the average annual poor rate raised in the Union parishes for 3 years ending Easter 1835 and therefore met the borrowing conditions of the Poor Law Commissioners. The River poorhouse and land was valued at £2,262 11s., comprising freehold land worth £302, buildings £1,320, furniture £365 4s 6d., fixtures £ 95 6s. 6d. Tenders for the new building ranged from £3,608 to £3,928, thus exceeding the £3,000 budget. In something of a quandary the Guardians asked Sir Francis whether they should sell River Workhouse and build elsewhere for 500 inmates similar to that at Bridge. Subsequently, Mr. Phipps, owner of River Paper Mill, offered to buy River Workhouse at valuation. The Poor Law Commissioners approved the sale and the intention to build elsewhere. In fact the River property stood vacant until 1843 when it was sold for £1400 to the founders of Hofwyl College. The main house, converted to a private house known as River House, is still standing today minus its original top storey.

An offer of 2½ acres of land from John Finnis for £300 in Buckland Bottom was accepted and tenders were invited for a workhouse for 500 based upon the Bridge Workhouse plans. Only a few days later a major problem arose when a solicitor threatened a trespass action on anybody acting on behalf of River Union attempting to use a certain road to reach the building plot. Mr. Finnis could not guarantee a right of way from Buckland Road. The Guardians quickly decided not to confirm the land purchase from Mr. Finnis, but to buy land offered by George Hatton (3 acres and 3 roods) in Buckland at £80 an acre plus the leasing of a further acre and one rood and 8 perches for 21 years at £2 10s. an acre.

Building tenders were invited by 11 July, only eight days later!

The tenders came in on time and that of John Finnis, carpenter, and Messrs. Collyer and Winder, bricklayers, to build for £4,381 was accepted. The Guardians then applied to the Commissioners to borrow £5,300, still not exceeding the average of the combined poor rates in the last three years. One week later the clerk was asked to write to parish overseers requesting that they order all able-bodied labourers on poor relief to report to Mr. Laud's farmyard opposite Buckland Brewery at 8am the next Thursday. Each was to be provided with a pick axe and possibly a wheelbarrow and to await instructions! Some fifty labourers then excavated and levelled the ground.

At a December 1835 meeting of the Guardians plans were displayed for an additional wash house and laundry plus an ironing room at an estimated cost of £135. In February 1836 it was agreed to purchase an additional five acres of land from George Laud at £80 an acre.

The new workhouse, replacing those at River and Martin, was eventually built at a total cost of £6,374 4s. 11d. and opened in 1836, having taken only nine months and one week to erect and fit. It was built as far away as possible from local residents; the nearest farm was Coombe Farm and the nearest house was half a mile away. It was built to the same plan as Bridge Workhouse in the form of a quadrangle with an entrance gate and two wings in front, low buildings and dormitories on the other three sides with walls across the yard to segregate the sexes and divide the old from the young. The Guardians' Board Room and the Master's Office were over the front entrance with a small hospital against the opposite wall. The resemblance to a prison was increased by having no windows looking outwards, only inwards. The Bridge buildings still survive today, although converted into dwellings.

The contents of the River workhouse were sold in August 1836, but Martin workhouse was hired for temporary use by the new union for one year at £20.

St. Mary's Parish joining the union necessitated the building of an infirmary on the bank behind the original workhouse. A loan of £2,000 was obtained for the purpose. The builders, Finnis, Collyer and Winder, submitted their bill on 19 October 1837 for £1864 19s. 8^{1}/2d. This building survives as Buckland Hospital's Ramsay and Churchill Wards. The Guardians received £2,107 15s. 9d. in 1838 from the sale of St. Mary's Parish poorhouse, which went toward repaying the loan for the new workhouse.

To meet demand there were further enlargements in 1849, 1871, 1897 and 1903. The greatest addition at any one time was that of 1897 when a loan of £5800 was raised. The chapel, which is now the Buckland Hospital staff dining room, was built through public subscription as was the laundry which continued in use until 1977, when the work was transferred to the new district laundry at the William Harvey Hospital.

Buckland Workhouse opens

The new workhouse at Buckland opened to receive paupers on 24 March 1836 and the first inmates were moved there from River on 22nd April that year. This was not without incident as an old man named Young from Ringwould Parish died whilst being moved. He did not seem unwell when he climbed into the wagon in which the old and infirm were transported from River 'but showed symptoms of drowsiness which proved to be the stupor of dissolution for, on arrival at the new workhouse after the rest of the party had alighted, the driver tried to rouse him when he was found to be quite dead.'

Inmates

There were four types of inmate: casuals or tramps, the able-bodied, the aged and the sick. A tramp could apply for admission between 4 and 9pm. He was asked his name, his age and birthplace, where he had come from and where he was going. He was given a bath, a meal of bread and soup, a bed and kept for one day during which he was employed by the Labour Master in gardening, breaking stones or chopping railway sleepers into firewood. The next day he was dismissed with a hunk of bread and cheese and a way ticket, entitling him to a free drink at a specified place halfway to the next workhouse. Able-bodied men, whether idle or unfortunate, could stay if they worked, but their wives and children were accommodated separately. Men did gardening, chopped wood and broke stones. Women cleaned, mended and washed clothes. Children were taught in the workhouse. The aged were allowed to stay for the rest of their lives, if necessary. The sick went to the workhouse infirmary.

Visitors had to have an order signed by the Parish Guardian and were only allowed 20 minutes a visit on Tuesday or Saturday except for sickness when the Governor could use his discretion.

The number in the institution in September 1843 was 286, made up of 89 men, 94 women, 46 boys under 16 and 57 girls under 16. Twenty years later, the *Dover Express* reported on 17 May 1872 that for the week ending 9 May there were 343 inmates at the beginning of the week and 18 newcomers during the week, one had died and 23 were discharged leaving 337. In addition 66 mendicants i.e. beggars were admitted. During the same week 1,396 people received outdoor relief at a total cost of £128 8s. 8d.

Outdoor relief

In April 1836 on instruction from Mr. Tufnell, the new Assistant Commissioner, outdoor relief to able-bodied paupers not having more than two children ceased, except in cases of sickness, accident or other emergency. In July it was agreed that 2s. 6d. a week should be the maximum outdoor relief for old paupers.

At that time loans were also made e.g. £2 to Widow Knott at St. Margaret's to enable her to open a small shop, £4 to Elizabeth Ellis of Charlton to recover goods seized for rent, £2 17s. to Susan Wilson of Charlton to buy a copper grate and 9s. 10d. to William Friend of Westcliffe to buy a coffin for his wife.

Workhouse Records

The admissions registers give details of the date, name age, occupation, on whose authority admitted, the place of settlement and observations such as: infirm, single, able-bodied, a dumb idiot, weak in mind, wife and children of, returned from gaol, bastard aged 5. Occupations included carpenter, cordwainer, servant, labourer and a German beggar.

From the discharge registers it appears that those who left had usually stayed in the workhouse for three or four weeks. Reasons for discharge include: 'to work in paper mill,' 'to live with …,' 'to harvesting,' 'committed to St. Augustine's,' 'departed this life,' 'removed to lunatic asylum,' 'deserted this house,' 'his own request,' 'committed to St. Augustine's Gaol by George Stringer Esq. for refusing to work.'

The Union's register of births reveals that there were about ten to twenty every year and all illegitimate. As expected the religious creed register shows most inmates as Anglican with a few nonconformists. Deaths in the workhouse were frequent, mostly of the aged, but with a few in the prime of life and some young children. In 1878 there were 63 deaths and 69 in 1880. The number of tramps admitted from June 1875 to May 1876 was 728 compared with 1,664 for the same period a year later.

Children's education

Early action was taken regarding the education of the workhouse children. An advertisement was placed in the local newspapers in April 1836 for a live-in schoolmaster and mistress at a combined salary of £60 a year plus heating and candles. They were to be of middle age without family with the task of instructing the workhouse children and would also be expected to make themselves generally useful. The same advertisement also sought a young, strong and healthy porter at 15 shillings a week. John and Elizabeth Mutton were appointed as teachers, but in September 1836 the schoolmaster was sacked for irregular conduct and the schoolmistress was suspended for inefficiency. Henry and Ann Iggulsden replaced them. Less than a year later there were several complaints against them from paupers, alleging beating of children as well as the schoolmistress making shirts for profit with the forced aid of the children. She begged forgiveness and was allowed to take in work provided it did not interfere with her duties. Then the workhouse master and mistress complained about them not attending to their duties and, following an investigation, they were all reprimanded and guidance rules issued.

In March 1838 the workhouse children were examined by the Guardians who told the schoolmaster and mistress that the children were a great credit to them. Only a couple of months later the schoolmistress was accused of not performing her duties satisfactorily, for her bad temper and for making charges against the Master which were entirely disproved. She was suspended and reported to the Commissioners for dismissal. They asked her to resign, but she refused and was dismissed. The new schoolmistress was Ann Blake at a salary of £20 a year plus heat and candles.

Apprenticeships

The cost of keeping children in the workhouse was reduced by apprenticing older boys and putting girls into domestic service. Following a direction from the Commissioners, in 1836 the Guardians resolved that no payments would be made for apprentices or those going into service, except for providing a suit of clothes. The Commissioners had commented, 'Premiums of £5 was too much, especially to so undesirable a trade as a chimney sweep.'

Food

Dinner on Christmas Day 1836 included baked beef and plum pudding for all the inmates and this was repeated in 1837 on the day of Queen Victoria's coronation. On this occasion the Board agreed to provide one pint of porter for each inmate to drink the Queen's health, which was paid for by subscription. This set a precedent for the next Christmas Day!

From reported deliveries it seems that about 150 loaves a day were delivered in 1837 at a cost of 5½d. a loaf. During the same year boneless beef, mutton and suet at 5s. 9d. a stone (14lbs.) or 4½d. per lb was bought.

In August 1837 the Board accepted the Medical Officer's recommended diets for those in the infirmary, but the Chairman later persuaded the Board to reconsider, which then decided to adopt the Poor Law Commission's dietary plan, which the Medical Officer could alter as he saw fit! By March 1846 the diet of the aged and infirm was augmented by 1½ ounces of tea and 4 ounces of sugar a week for women, but only 1 ounce of tea and 4 ounces of sugar for men for some reason!

Apparently in 1849 some paupers were entering the workhouse on Saturdays in order to receive the benefit of the Sunday dinner of meat pudding. The Poor Law Commission suggested altering the diet for casual poor and vagrants – instead of 20 ounces of meat pudding and vegetables, they should have 7 ounces of bread and 1 ounce of cheese for Sunday dinner!

Other matters

In May 1836 the Board allowed the Chaplain £6 10s. to buy religious books for the inmates and at the same meeting ordered boots: mens' at 7 shillings a pair, boys' at 5 shillings, women's at 4 shillings and men's high boots at 5 shillings. A mangle was also to be acquired at no more than £16. The proposed annual salary for the Chaplain of £50 had to be reduced to £40 to bring it into line with other unions. The auditor's salary was agreed at £25.

Ursula Tonbridge, a pauper, had acted as unpaid nurse and in May 1837 the Board decided to employ her in the infirmary at 5 shillings a week plus two workhouse rations. Two years later, however, in 1839 she was found guilty of immorality and discharged.

The Board objected when it received a bill for window and land tax from the Collector of Taxes, but was not supported by the Poor Law Commissioners. January 1838 brought many applications for relief from the able bodied due to the bad weather and the Guardians asked the Surveyor to use them on highways work where possible.

Six months later the Guardians took steps to reduce the ever increasing costs and agreed that pensioners and others with means but unable to look after themselves should be charged 3s. 6d. a week for living in the workhouse. At the same meeting they decided to get tougher with those men whose mothers and daughters were in the workhouse whom they could probably support themselves.

Inmates were allowed leave of absence of up to two days, but the master complained in 1839 about the inconvenience of inmates returning from leave of absence after 9pm. It was agreed that they should be back by 8pm or lose the privilege.

Financial irregularities

A discrepancy of £262 11s. 2d. was found in the workhouse accounts in 1839. William Hill, the Collector (of the poor rate) who was paid no salary but 4d. in the pound of what he collected, was suspended and asked to make up the deficiency. He was taken into custody and his chattels sold for £8 12s. 9d. as part payment of the deficiency. The four gentlemen who had stood as Mr. Hills' surety when he was appointed had to pay the balance. A similar irregularity occurred in 1847 when Henry Mutton, Collector and Relieving Officer for Hougham was sacked and convicted by the magistrates for a deficiency of £284 3s. His sureties, Revd. J. Monins and George Ledger had to make good the shortfall.

Staff salaries in 1849

The quarterly salaries in 1849 for workhouse staff were: chaplain £10, clerk £31 5s., master £20, relieving officers (2) £38 15s., collector £22 10s., schoolmaster £7 10s., schoolmistress £6 5s., porter £12, inspector of nuisances £12 10s. and the various medical officers: George Rutley £25, R Hunt £12 10s., John Walter, and Frederick Chalk £6 5s.

Disease strikes

Dover, in common with the rest of the country, suffered a cholera epidemic in 1849 and on 28 December there were 83 cases of cholera and 188 cases of diarrhoea in the workhouse. The agreed price for the doctor's examination was 10 shillings for cholera cases and 4 shillings for diarrhoea.

Emigration

Some paupers were encouraged to migrate to the industrial north and were given £3 to £5 for furniture and clothing. Others were assisted to emigrate to Canada and Australia with sums ranging from £20 to £30. Emigration was not always popular, however, for in 1847 one of six paupers taken to London and put on board ship went ashore and deliberately broke a pane of glass. Brought before the magistrate, he was given the choice of jail for one month or emigrating. He chose jail! Another jumped ship. More typical was 20 February 1850 when a man and wife and their six children plus a widow and two children left the workhouse to start a new life overseas.

20th century

More comfortable conditions existed in the workhouse by the beginning of the 20th century as a lengthy article showed in the *Dover Express* in 1902. At the time Mr. Sandercock had been the master for 18 years and Mrs. Sandercock the matron. Both had enjoyed very good reputations in their posts with 25 years 'in the business.' There were 427 inmates made up of 131 men and 71 women aged over 60 as well as 58 temporarily disabled able-bodied men under 60 and two in health. Of the children 33 were boys between 9 and 16, 13 boys between 2 and 9, 35 girls between 9 and 16, 19 between 2 and 9 plus 12 infants under 2 years old. The reporter commented that there were only four able-bodied women and two men, which was good, but meant that much of the maintenance work of the house had to be paid for, leading to increased expenditure!

The article included a tour of the premises. Old men occupied the south side (an original part of the building) with a large yard and seats all round off which there was a dining hall, which also served as a day room. It was large enough for them all, warm and well ventilated. On the same level for those who found the stairs difficult was a bedroom. The main dormitories were three or four very long rooms, all scrupulously clean with whitewashed walls. Some inmates had separate rooms. On the opposite side of the yard were old women, looking picturesque in their tartan shawls, gowns and aprons, all busy. There was work for everybody capable, including women making shirts and frocks which staff had cut out and machined. The workroom was pleasant with windows giving good views of the Dover hills and with pictures on the walls and rugs on the floor. The other sides of the quadrangle were for the old infirm with special attendants and a doctor who called daily. The nursery was a good sized room. The older children were eating bread and beef tea at a table and the younger ones were cradled and sucking on bottles. Several prams in the promenading ground had kindly been donated by townspeople, since the Guardians could not possibly justify their purchase.

The kitchen was a modern building near the entrance with a large gas range and an oven capable of roasting a whole pig with a few joints on the side, but, 'this not being a pork day, it was out of use with an assistant inside scouring it.' There was a large machine for making beef tea plus three large tea boilers. Dinner consisted of legs of mutton cooked under steam pressure in a Benham cooker – a tall iron chest divided into two compartments, one containing 14 legs of mutton and the other puddings and potatoes in their jackets. Inmates did the cooking supervised by the cook. The menu for a week was:

Mondays	mutton
Tuesdays	bacon with rice and milk
Wednesdays	soup with boiled rice
Thursday	roast pork with rice pudding
Fridays	fish
Saturdays	Irish stew
Sundays	roast beef

Mrs. Sandercock and the laundress were in charge of the laundry, which handled 12,000 items a week. The machinery was not apparently equal to the work – two powered washing machines and one operated by hand. Work had doubled in the last five years. It comprised sorting, washing, rinsing and drying. After going through some sort of wet extractor, the clothes were put out to dry and then went into the ironing and mangling room after which they were aired in a warm linen store and then sorted for their various destinations.

In the provision store were bins of rice, barley, haricot beans, cheese, bread and biscuits. Biscuits had only been allowed by the considerate Local Government Board in the last two years – for the children only – with a daily ration of two ounces a day. The master's practice was to give half the ration at lunchtime and the other half before they went to bed.

In the clothing store the matron and her two paid assistants with help from the women made all the clothes for the inmates, except the men's and boys' suits, including frocks for the girls and pinafores for the children. They also did all the necessary mending. Boots were bought by contract but mended by a shoemaker on the premises. Boys' clothing was mended by a workhouse tailor and some of the boys were taught the trade.

Skilled able-bodied men admitted to the workhouse were put to good use, repairing, painting and making cupboards etc. The excellent state of the decoration and furniture was testimony to their skills.

Dr. Cooper Fenn was the medical officer and Miss Foster the superintendent nurse. On arrival at the workhouse the doctor would ring the dispensary bell to alert the inmates who wished to see him. Some of the sick were admitted to the hospital which overlooked the workhouse on the higher ground. There were separate wards for women and men. At the rear was the padded room, which, fortunately, was not used very often. At this time the hospital buildings were being extended, including a lying-in ward and nurses' accommodation. These were not included in the original plans, since it was then thought that a few old paupers acting as ward men and women with the master and matron looking in occasionally would be sufficient, but now there were twelve paid nurses.

A chapel for Church of England services had been built at some stage by public subscription and the Vicar of Buckland, Revd. Turberville Evans, was the chaplain.

No longer were children of school age taught in the workhouse. Instead they attended the local schools, the girls at Buckland and the boys at Charlton. Whilst this was evidence of enlightenment, the children were still obviously from the workhouse with their shaven heads and grim garments.

In the workhouse they were looked after by the industrial trainers, Miss Whitham and Mr. Mason. There were other signs of improvements in facilities and attitudes. During the tour there were 47 boys and 55 girls in the large and pretty dining hall for dinner and they were not dressed as pauper children. After dinner they went to play with their toys in the toy rooms. There were swings in the yard and the children were drilled to music on a harmonium. The girls' bedroom was very neat, tidy and clean with beds down each side and cots down the middle. There was also a kitchen where the girls were taught to cook to help them when they went into service.

Expenditure, particularly the cost of food, was discussed with the Master.

Apparently a new diet with the 'more solid part consisting of legs of mutton and boneless beef' had resulted in a very great reduction in the butcher's bill. Costs for meat under the old and new diet were compared:

	1901	1902
Beef	£1,038	£ 818
Mutton	£ 555	£ 268
Total	£1,593	£1,086

This was not a clear saving since the new diet brought expense in other areas: pork £116 more, bacon £161 more, milk £141 more, the new biscuit ration £61, jam for the old and children £42. The costs of butter and margarine were down by £78 10s. 5d. The reporter was told that the Local Government Board bread allowance was nearly double the amount actually needed. As a consequence the master put out half the allowance initially at each meal and then, during the meal, asked who wanted more, but there were very few takers. Apparently 10,000lbs. of bread had been returned to store for future use. Even so 6,000lbs. of bread a year was wasted, although this was fed to pigs and came back as pork! The master was determined to save most of the wastage. The total cost of food in the past year, £4,852 compared with the previous year of £4,738, was an increase of only £113 despite the new diet and the extra numbers accommodated. The total cost of the workhouse in the last year was £9,491 compared with £9,500 in the previous twelve months. Much of the expenditure was not really for the poor but for County Council expenditure for lunatics and the increased cost of nursing lumped into the Poor Rate, but over which the Guardians had no control.

The newspaper reporter concluded that there was no case for going back to buying cases of mutton or quarters of beef. Foreign meat might be tried if patriotism permitted! He felt, however, that these unfortunate people, boxed up without choice and with no say over what they ate or how they exercised, needed good, wholesome food. Good food was not very much more expensive than the inferior article and might be better in the long run. There was praise for the Guardians and the staff, 'It would not be possible in the Poor Law Unions of England to find a better record.'

Christmas Day in the workhouse

On 1 January 1904 the *Dover Express* reported on the 1903 Christmas Day in the workhouse where there were 510 inmates. 'The master, John Sandercock, had decorated the wards of the house, the infirmary, the schoolroom, entrance halls and board room with a large quantity of evergreens, which looked very festive. Members of the Board of Guardians visited, including Matthew Pepper, Chairman, plus several other ladies and gentlemen to assist. The chairman toured the wards and spoke cheering words and distributed a new sixpenny piece to each child. He then addressed the inmates and thanked the visitors for giving up their time. Christmas dinner comprised: 600lbs. of roast beef, 600lbs. of plum pudding, 2 barrels of ale and 216 bottles of mineral waters. For dessert there was a box of oranges, 30lbs. of apples, 56lbs. figs, 56lbs. dates, 2½ bushels of mixed nuts, 28lbs. sweets, 56lbs. finger nuts, 50lbs. of cake and 150 bananas. Old men received 1 ounce of tobacco and old women who wanted it, snuff! Various gifts were distributed from well wishers in the town: 1 case of oranges, magazines and scrap books, 8 ounces of tobacco, 64lbs. sugar, 64½lbs. tea, toys, three boxes of prize packets, dolls, toys etc., one case of oranges, tea and sugar, 38½lbs. tea and 38lbs. sugar, Christmas cards, two games, toys, illustrated papers, pictures, 36 half pound bags of sugar, 36 quarter pound bags of tea and 36 packets of sweets, cakes, oranges and figs, sweets and oranges, 100 oranges, tobacco and sweets for the children. Mr. A. H. Pointer, dressed as Father Christmas, went round the rooms laden with toys. In the evening there was a grand concert by the Sunflower Minstrels for all who could move from the wards both male and female. Old

ELECTION OF GUARDIANS, 1908.

To the Parochial Electors of the Parish of Hougham.

Ladies and Gentlemen,

At the request of a large number of Electors I have been nominated for the Office of Guardian. If elected I shall make it my earnest study to carry out the Poor Law in a sympathetic manner, and at the same time to prevent any unnecessary extravagance.

In Imperial Politics (which these local Elections so much influence) I am a Conservative, strongly in favour of Religious Education ; and, although not a faddist, a supporter of Temperance in all things, but opposed to all measures of Confiscation.

Hoping that I may be favoured with your support,

I have the honour to be,

Ladies and Gentlemen,

Your very obedient Servant,

Notice for the election of Guardians in 1908

men, old women and young women wards were visited by the troupe of minstrels and their efforts to amuse the inmates were very successful. The day ended with cheers and thanks from all the inmates to the Guardians and officers.'

The editor commented that the sick, the infirm, the aged and children made up the greater proportion of inmates and that there were very few paupers in Dover. There were no savings to be made in the workhouse but possibly some in outdoor relief.

Demon drink

Inmates being the 'worse for wear' was not unknown. The *Dover Express* reported in January 1905 that the master of the workhouse had locked-up three inmates after they returned drunk and on 7 April 1905 the newspaper reported that Samuel Baker, a resident of Dover Workhouse, said to be 'well behaved when sober but a demon when drunk,' appeared before magistrates for the seventieth time and was given 21 days hard labour.

Uruguay's vice-consul, who lived at 7 Leyburne Terrace in Dover, raised some hackles in 1905 when he refused to pay his Poor Rate because he claimed his home was part of Uruguay's territory, even though his office was in Folkestone, and therefore not part of Dover. Magistrates rejected his claim!

In 1909 the Guardians agreed to take into the workhouse any children detained under the 1908 Children Act for various crimes. This cost the town council 7s. 6d. a child although the government paid 5s. 3d. In 1913 the Guardians decided that all children over the age of three should be boarded out.

With the outbreak of the First World War numbers in the workhouse dropped from 600 in 1914 to 300 in 1915 and those receiving outdoor relief were fewer. Costs were not greatly reduced, however, due to the increased cost of food. By 1924 the Board of Guardians needed £50,000 for the year, although this was less than the previous year. Dover was affected by the 1926 General Strike and the Board of Guardians helped the wives and families of strikers, but had to raise loans to do so. At other times the Guardians relieved those unemployed who were not entitled to the 'dole'. In 1929 the Guardians, on orders from the Ministry of Health, put some able-bodied men on relief clearing up the town's rubbish dump at Coombe Farm.

Public Assistance Institution

The Board of Guardians continued running the workhouse until 1930 when Kent County Council took over responsibility under the 1929 Local Government Act. There was a County Public Assistance Committee with local Guardians' Committees. Dover came under the South East Guardians' Committee. The workhouses were still run by the master, matron and relieving officers. The post of Clerk to the Board of Guardians was abolished but the post of Deputy Public

Dover Workhouse in 1935

Dover workhouse in the 1930s before partial demolotion

Demolition of part of Dover Workhouse in 1936 with chapel in the background

Demolition of part of Dover Workhouse in 1936

Assistance Officer was created instead. One of the earliest decisions of the new authority was to demolish the original workhouse and to replace it with what is now the lower block of the hospital or, as it was called then, the Public Assistance Institution. Work started in 1934 and finished in 1936.

Outdoor relief was still being paid in that decade. By 1934 it totalled £29,000 – treble the 1931 total. This was no doubt a reflection of mass unemployment at the time due to the collapse of the world economy.

Mr. Vickery's memories

Mr. G. Vickery, an Assistant Administrator at Buckland Hospital, who retired in 1984, wrote his recollections of his many years at the hospital, including the pre-war years as a public assistance institution.

'The Pathology Department was the porters' lodge. There was always a gate porter on duty who recorded the name of every person who entered or left the building together with the time of arrival and departure. The Surgical Wards housed the able-bodied male inmates. These were normally employed on labouring duties or in the garden. The present car park and the hillside were cultivated and at one time pigs were kept both for sale and in order to provide the Christmas dinner. The X-Ray Department housed the stores. Stock control was very strict and replacement made only on production of the broken or worn out item. Children were accommodated in the present pharmacy which also included a two bed maternity ward. Able-bodied women were accommodated in the present Accident Department. These ladies were employed on domestic duties in the kitchen and in the laundry. The male chronic sick were accommodated in what are now Ramsay and Churchill wards and female patients in the other blocks. A magnificent padded cell was demolished to create the patio outside Churchill Ward day room and the generator house behind the maternity ward was the mortuary.

The Institution was administered by a master and matron who enjoyed good job protection as they could not be dismissed without the permission of the Home Secretary. These were normally joint appointments and it was essential for any ambitious clerk to marry a State Registered Nurse. The majority of staff were required to be resident and all worked very long hours. Clerks, who worked the shortest hours, were on duty from 9am to 5pm and on alternate days assisted in the Casual Ward from 5pm to 9pm. A half day off was given on alternate Saturdays and a day off on alternate Sundays. On Sunday the duty clerk was required to pump the organ at church services which were compulsory for all able-bodied inmates. For this, as a clerk, I received 7s. 6d. a week 'plus full residential emoluments', which included a blue three piece suit with two pairs of trousers a year.

The menu for inmates did not vary from week to week except on Christmas Day. There were two diets, normal and light. The portions were decided by reference to a printed schedule, for example I remember that beef pudding, which was served on one day a week, comprised a fixed amount of 'clods and stickings' (suet, flour and water) multiplied by the number of portions. The staff were divided into messes each of which decided its own menu. Ingredients were purchased from local shops against a very generous cash allocation which permitted a high standard of living. Cooks were employed to prepare meals, one in the Nurses' Home for the nursing staff and one in the kitchen for the other messes.

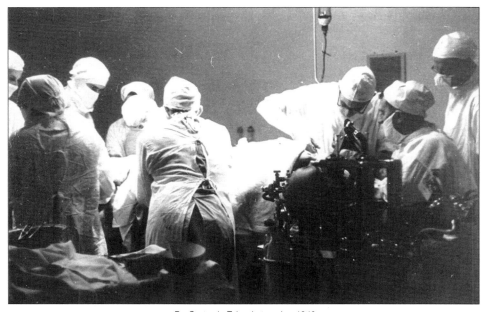

Dr. Gertrude Toland at work c.1940

The Second World War saw the start of the transition to a general hospital. All the able-bodied inmates were transferred to other institutions. The lower block was designated an Emergency Medical Service hospital and Colonel Birdwood was appointed Medical Superintendent. An operating theatre was installed in the present recovery room and wards equipped to receive the expected air-raid casualties. The rooms over the Accident Department were used to provide accommodation for the members of the Volunteer Auxiliary Detachment (VAD) directed to work at the hospital. A gas decontamination centre was built in front of the main block, which was later demolished. An air-raid shelter was built in the area between the operating theatre and chapel and a large public underground shelter erected in the area to the east of the present entrance to the car park. During the period of the 'phoney war' the hospital was used to treat both military and civilian sick. My main memory of this period is of the large number of tonsil and adenoid operations performed. Following the German invasion of Holland and Belgium in May 1940, all the civilian sick were evacuated and the hospital prepared to receive casualties from the continent. It was not long before British, French and Belgian casualties started to arrive and, until the end of the Dunkirk evacuation, teams of surgeons worked twenty-four hours a day in the operating theatre and the VADs ceased to be bored. The routine was for the seriously wounded to be admitted, operated on and then transferred to other hospitals.

After the Dunkirk evacuation preparations were made to meet the expected invasion. A restriction was placed on the movement of civilians and all the chronic sick were evacuated. The Casual Wards were turned into an Air Raid Precaution post. The present medical wards were taken over by the army and used as a military hospital. The lower block was used for civilian patients under the EMS scheme but in 1943 administration was taken over by the Public Health Department of Kent County Council and the name changed to Dover County Hospital.'

The hospital staff did outstanding work particularly during the Dunkirk evacuation period and Dr. Gertrude Toland was one of the heroes of that time.'

Mr. Vickery added, 'In the late 1950s one of my tasks was to sort through and dispose of the effects of the casualties which had been kept in the stores and these included an alarming quantity of ammunition of all calibres, dehydrated cigarettes, spirits which had lost their alcohol content but, surprisingly, very few personal items.'

With the introduction of the National Health Service in 1948 control was transferred to the Regional Hospital Board of S. E. Hospital Management Committee and the hospital's name was changed to Buckland Hospital.

Chapter 6

DEVELOPMENT OF DOVER'S HOSPITAL AND WELFARE SERVICES

Whilst services for the poor and aged were being improved, a dual system of charity and payment developed to treat the seriously ill. In addition, provision to contain the incidence of infectious diseases which periodically swept across the country was financed originally by charity but subsequently by the community. Environmentally, by the 20th century Dover was apparently one of the better places to live or visit, particularly if you had money. In 1905 a national magazine claimed that Dover was one of the top seaside health resorts on the south coast. In 1923 the death rate in Dover was 10.3 per 1000 which was apparently very low for the time.

People's Dispensary

As early as 1823 a dispensary, providing medical treatment, opened in Dover under the patronage of the Earl of Liverpool, Prime Minister and Lord Warden of the Cinque Ports, but this lapsed for lack of funds. It was revived in 1828 by the Duke of Wellington and was relocated off the Market Square, but subsequently moved to Snargate Street and eventually to Queen Street. It was funded by local worthies for the benefit of the sick poor. Those contributing a guinea were made Governors and for ten guineas one could become a Life Governor. An apothecary was appointed at £80 a year who lived in with 'coals and candles provided.' In the first year 452 patients were treated, some in their own homes. Of these, 311 were said to be cured, 35 relieved and 23 dying. Eleven of the deaths were due to consumption; the rest were due to palsy, apoplexy, dropsy, 'water in the chest' and 'water in the head,' it is recorded.

Royal Victoria Hospital

In 1850 it was resolved to augment the dispensary with a hospital. In the early part of that year when a cholera epidemic was subsiding in England the people of Dover raised a fund to establish a Dover hospital as a thanksgiving for having escaped the epidemic. £1,760 was raised and Brook House in the High Street, which was for sale at the time, was acquired for £1,336. This Brook House, not to be confused with the building of the same name which once stood in Maison Dieu Road, was a private residence built by Alderman Dickenson, papermaker, for his own use and subsequently occupied by the Dowager Lady Knatchbull and in 1839 by the Dowager Lady Suffield. After some alterations to the building the hospital was opened on 1 May 1851. Mr. and Mrs. Jarrett were appointed porter and matron at £45 a year. A female servant was later allowed at £25 a year. There were only nine beds. Running costs in the first year were £125. Under Rule 16 patients were asked to give thanks in their own church when cured. Meadows surrounded the hospital but when these were sold as building land a further half an acre was purchased in 1858 at a cost of £740.

It was proposed to move the hospital to another site in 1870 and again in 1897 it was suggested that a new building should be erected between Laureston Place and Ashen Tree Lane. However, it was decided to utilise the land already owned and a fund was raised by local subscription to build a new wing as a permanent memorial to Queen Victoria. King Edward VII allowed the enlarged building to be named the Royal Victoria Hospital. There were later additions and it became a busy general hospital and training school for nurses. New nurses' quarters were opened in 1915.

The First World War with its frequent air raids brought extra casualties and pressure on beds. In 1917 the Red House in London Road, River, was taken over and used as a relief hospital. In the same year matters were made worse by the Crabble tram accident when 11 of the casualties remained in hospital for a considerable time.

Finance was always a problem and was raised in a variety of ways including collecting boxes in public houses and work places as well as spontaneous donations – for instance for skating on Frith Pond. The Hospital Saturday Fund was introduced with a parade on the seafront. Pound Day collections began in 1903. The first Hospital Fete was held in 1924 in Dover College grounds, but it ran into trouble after a couple of years when it was reported for including tombola. The fete was abandoned, but resumed in 1929 without tombola! In 1930 there was a big effort to raise half a million shillings to pay for an extension. This was started in 1933, providing additional wards and nurses' quarters at a cost of £8,000.

In 1938 an appeal for £20,000 for a nursing home and modernisation of the hospital kitchen raised only £400. Instead, the Coleman Trustees leased The Shrubbery on Crabble Hill as a home for 30 nurses with the rent being used for convalescence away from Dover.

Royal Victoria Hospital c.1910

Isolation or Fever Hospital, Noah's Ark

At the outbreak of the Second World War the in-patient facilities were evacuated to Waldershare Park, the Coleman Nurses' Home became a military hospital and the old workhouse became a Casualty Hospital.

Fever Hospital

In about 1871 Dr. Astley established a small fever hospital on Chapel Mount (Noah's Ark) in a former farmhouse. This hospital proved invaluable during the smallpox epidemic of 1872 and additional accommodation was added. Eventually, the doctor handed over the whole establishment to the corporation which at that time was the urban sanitary authority. The Fever Hospital was in the news in 1914 when a nurse made a series of allegations. The master and matron resigned even though an enquiry exonerated them. Later, all the staff were replaced. The reconstruction and modernisation of the Isolation Hospital, as it had become known, started in 1926.

The corporation added further blocks and made improvements until at the beginning of the Second World War there were two blocks for the treatment of infectious diseases, one for tuberculosis and one for poliomyelitis. In addition the corporation purchased a further building about a mile and a half away in the Poulton Valley for the treatment of smallpox.

Other developments

In the period 1900 to 1918 there were a number of government measures to improve the health and well-being of the population in general and particularly the poor. The poor health of the young men recruited for the Boer War led to legislation in 1906 that enabled local authorities to provide school meals. Medical examinations of school children followed in 1907. The new National Health Insurance Act came into force in 1912. A local consequence was that all Dover doctors refused to implement the scheme and those attached to Friendly Societies resigned. This happened throughout the country. More government legislation in 1914 enabled grants to be made to local authorities for nursing and clinical services especially to address the high infant mortality rate with help for antenatal and child care clinics, home visitors and food for mothers and children in need. Like everywhere else, the people of Dover suffered severely from the 1918-1919 influenza epidemic, evidenced by the many announcements of death in issues of the *Dover Express*.

After the First World War ex-soldiers' organisations became very active. In 1919 a Veterans' Club opened in Liverpool Street and Comrades of the Great War opened a club in a Waterloo Crescent house. These clubs provided support for the war injured and the many who were unable to find unemployment.

Dover's population was falling. The 1921 census showed a total of 39,985 compared with 43,645 in 1911. This drop was probably due to a combination of the absence of the garrison at this time, lack of work and the non-return of seafront people after the War.

A maternity and infant welfare clinic in part of Brook House was opened in 1922 by the French Minister of Health! Infant mortality at this time was 50 per 1,000 born. In 1923 Major Astor, the MP for Dover, offered to provide a building close to Brook House in Maison Dieu Road for use as a dental clinic and to pay the costs for three years. It opened as the Astor Clinic in 1924. In fact Major Astor maintained the clinic until 1942 when it was handed over to the town. An important national development in 1936 was the introduction of the visiting

Brook House, Maison Dieu Road in 1989

District Nurse service. Locally, two nurses were appointed initially with another two later.

Ambulance services

Before any organised ambulance service was introduced it usually fell to the police, who were trained in first aid, to get the injured and sick to hospital, using stretchers. These were sited in various parts of the town with fire fighting equipment. By the end of the 19th century Furley Litters were introduced – covered stretchers on wheels – which were still in use in the 1930s. The town also

A Furley Litter in 1922

Crossley ambulance in 1924

possessed a horse-drawn fever wagon with bunks for transporting patients to the Fever Hospital. The local St. John Ambulance Brigade obtained its first Furley Litter in 1906 and its first motor ambulance in 1924 – albeit secondhand. This was the town's ambulance service until the National Health Service was introduced after the Second World War.

After 1945

Following the end of hostilities in 1945 planning commenced to meet the need for improved hospital facilities in the town. Because of the increasing cost of treatment the voluntary subscriptions and income from patients were insufficient to cover the cost of running the Royal Victoria Hospital and additional funds were provided by Kent County Council. One result of this joint funding was that the two hospital establishments in Dover, the Royal Victoria and the County Hospital at Buckland, co-operated to provide a comprehensive acute medical service. As a first stage the Matron of the Royal Victoria Hospital was asked to include Buckland in her nursing duties and both hospitals were used for nurse training.

There were only two beds at the Royal Victoria Hospital for maternity cases and two at Buckland and very limited facilities for children. In order to meet the pressing need of the area to accommodate these specialities work commenced on upgrading the old infirmary at Buckland.

National Health Service

The 5th July, 1948 was perhaps the most significant date in the history of health care in this country and Dover in particular. On that day the National Health Service came into being and locally the Minister of Health became responsible for the County Hospital, providing general medicine, gynaecology and ENT (ears, nose and throat) beds with at that time the maternity and children's wards under construction; the Royal Victoria Hospital, providing general and orthopaedic surgery beds together with an out-patient and casualty service; the Noah's Ark Isolation Hospital, providing a ward each for infectious diseases and poliomyelitis; and Poulton Hospital, providing beds for smallpox and cholera.

The Royal Victoria ceased to be supported by local voluntary efforts. The Hospital Workers' Fund was wound up, having raised £70,000 since 1917 and the Hospital Linen League became the Additional Comforts League. Ron Proudler, a local dentist, took an initiative in 1955 which led to the formation of the League of Friends of Dover Hospitals to provide comforts for patients. Its first annual garden party that year raised £400.

With the NHS now established the fund launched in 1945 to raise £250,000 for a Battle of Britain Memorial Hospital on the White Cliffs was no longer needed. It was wound up and much of the money raised was used to build the Battle of Britain Homes now facing York Street and administered by Dover Municipal Charities.

One of the first acts of the new administration was to attempt to remove all association with the Poor Laws and the County Hospital was renamed Buckland Hospital. The local authority co-operated by changing the name of the approach road from Union Road to Coombe Valley Road. The maternity ward was opened on the 1 February 1949 and the children's ward later that year.

In the early 1950s, following the creation of regional facilities at Dartford, the smallpox hospital was closed and the site sold. At about the same time the war damaged block at the Isolation Hospital was demolished. Plans were prepared to utilize the unoccupied buildings at Buckland Hospital. Access to the upper block was either by a roadway or by a stone staircase. The first phase was to install lifts and upgrade the block at the eastern end to form new medical wards. This was completed in 1960 and the patients were moved from the lower block into the new wards. The next stage was to create better operating theatre facilities and upgrade the vacated medical wards to form a surgical unit. By 1961 the hospital had 220 beds. Two new operating theatres meant an end to operations at the Royal Victoria Hospital in 1964.

As rebuilding and expansion of Buckland Hospital occurred, more and more work was transferred from the Royal Victoria Hospital. Eventually it was left with only a stroke unit and geriatric day hospital and in 1987 its doors finally closed.

In the meantime the Isolation Hospital had been converted into an eye hospital, but it closed after 20 years in 1981 and Dover patients then had to travel to Folkestone.

With a national move to larger, regionalised, better equipped hospitals the 1990s brought reductions in the size and facilities available at Buckland with the closure of some wards, including the children's ward, reducing the number of beds from 221 to 100. The accident and emergency service was also lost, although a minor injuries unit survived and some specialist support services were introduced as well as a new birthing unit. By the end of 2005 the hospital had lost its post mortem facilities and its one remaining operating theatre. The general rundown in hospital facilities available in Dover caused considerable dismay to the local population forced as patients or visitors to travel to hospitals at Canterbury, Ashford or Margate.

We should not forget that amongst all these changes aimed at producing a better and more efficient health service for everybody were simultaneous moves to make hospitals more friendly places for patients and visitors alike: the patients' meals service with a choice of menu, visitors' restaurants, ward telephones, radios and television screens as well as cheerful furnishings – all a far cry from the spartan conditions of previous centuries in workhouses and infirmaries.

Chapter 7

CHARITABLE ORGANISATIONS

We have traced how religious institutions in mediaeval times bore the main burden of caring for the sick, the infirm and destitute until the Dissolution and then how the State, through various acts of parliament, required local parishes and later Boards of Guardians to assume the role. Running parallel with this gradual development of statutory provision and the associated poor rate, culminating with the introduction of the National Health Service, were the supplementary efforts of the Dover town council, associations, societies and charities as well as individuals.

Dover Almshouse Fund

In the 16th century there was a move toward supporting small almshouses rather than ancient hospitals. According to Revd. John Lyon's History of Dover the first almshouse for the destitute was in St. Nicholas ward, given by some charitable person prior to any formal relief of the poor. This may well have been for distressed soldiers and sailors and their wives. If they died, the charity buried them at sea and if they recovered they were sent on their journey as far as Buckland. In 1532 the Mayor agreed to exchange this almshouse for a house in St. George's ward and so the almshouse moved from a structure built over the river near Butchery Gate 'since time out of mind' to large premises in Queen Street (adjoining Market Lane), belonging to Oliver Lythgo, a former mayor. Robert Justice, who died in 1552, left 6s. 8d. toward a rebuild of the decaying premises, but this was not achieved until 1611 when the Mayor and Jurats lent £10 to enable the wardens to complete the work, using materials from St. Martin's church. It looked like a hospital with rows of beds partitioned off. The Mayor was master and two members of the Common Council were warden and treasurer. By 1588 the charity owned four donated houses fronting York Street, while Thomas Andrews, Mayor and MP, gave a house in 1599. In the same year Richard Toms donated land, followed by a similar donation in 1603 by George Bussey. Thomas Ellwood, Mayor and MP, gave £14 and a piece of land in 1612 and Thomas Badcock bequeathed £10 in 1610.

From surviving records we know that in 1629 annual income from property yielded £21 1s. In that year Mayor Luke Pepper was master of the almshouse and Valentine Tatnell and William Richards were the wardens. The almshouse owned 12 acres of arable land leased by Thomas Broom at Hougham for £12 a year plus a half acre at Cowgate with some dwellings at 30 shillings rent, a Biggin Street dwelling at £1 and two more with rent of 20 shillings in St. James' parish. Land at Paul's Corner, Charlton yielded £5 10s. and there was also land at Tilmanstone. From 1629 the charity catered not only for soldiers' and sailors' wives but foreigners, ex-prisoners of war, the sick, cripples, melancholy persons and smallpox victims, some of whom lived out. If they died, the charity paid for burial. The Cowgate cottages had fallen into decay by 1693 when the land was sold for £3.

Buck's 1737 Plan of Town and Harbour shows another almshouse next to 'The Buildings' on the N. E. side of the tidal harbour, but nothing else is known about it.

In 1800 income from property was £237 and St. Mary's overseers petitioned the corporation to allow the almshouse charity income to be used for Poor Law purposes, but the Lord Chancellor would not allow it and ordered that the accumulated funds of £1,657 be used to build additional homes for the aged and that any future surpluses were to be used similarly or to relieve the casual poor.

The records in 1812 show the fund's income and its sources:

Tilmanstone	3 fields	annual rent	£10
Hougham	1 field	annual rent	£21 10s.
Hougham	1 field	annual rent	£5 2s.
Charlton Bottom	1 field	annual rent	£21
Paul's Corner	1 field	annual rent	£51 1s.
Upwell	1 field	annual rent	£12
Piece of land in St. James' parish		annual rent	15s.
A cellar near the almshouse		annual rent	£2
Annuity on Biggin Street house		annual rent	£1
4 tenements		annual rent	£4
Annual interest from town on £150 loan			£6
Annual interest from £900 5% stock			£40 10s.
		Total	£174 18s.

York Street almshouses

When income exceeded expenditure the surplus was loaned to the corporation at 5% interest. When this was not possible and the corporation needed to borrow money elsewhere, the almshouse was used as security. In 1607 the corporation borrowed £50 at 5% interest and mortgaged the property as security. Another £50 was borrowed in 1755 and £100 in 1758. The corporation retained management of the almshouse fund until 1835 when, as a consequence of the Municipal Corporations Act, it was transferred to the Dover Almshouse Trustees and the debts had to be repaid. They had cost the corporation £760 in interest.

In 1822 Chancery decreed that the accumulated funds of the Dover Almshouse should be spent in erecting additional small almshouses for aged men and women and the existing houses should be fitted up with beds as formerly for the reception of poor afflicted persons. As a result, 20 houses, opened in 1824, were built in a square by the corporation from the Almshouse Fund behind the four existing almshouses in York Street.This necessitated the removal of one of the four original houses. Eleven more were built in 1841 on the south side of the square and a small chapel was added. The 50 inmates were chosen on the basis of half from St. Mary's Parish, a quarter from St. James' Parish, and an eighth each from Charlton and Hougham.

The Dover almshouse in Queen Street was used as a seamen's hospital for distressed mariners until 1872. The building was then sold in 1887 to Sir Richard Dickeson when its funds were transferred to the Dover Hospital (later the Royal Victoria Hospital) with a responsibility to retain some beds for seamen.

At the beginning of the 20th century the Dover Almshouse Trustees consisted of members of the Town Council and the Board of Guardians plus some co-opted members. The editor of the *Dover Express* in 8 January 1904 had something to say about the activities of the Almshouse Trustees. Apparently the Board of Guardians had stopped outdoor relief for some residents of Dover's almshouses and the Almshouse Trustees were to consider whether residents had sufficient means to maintain themselves without help from the Union. If not, relief should be reinstated. The editor gave his view: 'Trustees ought not to consider applications from residents with three or four shillings coming in. Almshouses are designed for people who are not absolute paupers. It is hopeless for private persons to make absolute provision for the destitute – that can only be done by the State via the Poor Law. Trustees in future should give help to 'broken down tradespeople or persons who have but a little left and are too aged and broken down to ever hope to get any more and should not look to the Poor Law to supplement provision.'

The 15 January 1904 edition of the same newspaper contained this editorial: 'After original foundation in mediaeval times Dover Almshouses were somewhat neglected until the 16th and 17th centuries when several benefactors gave them a fresh start. The present houses, built early 19th century with later improvements, have used up all revenue. Trustees have been able to offer inmates shelter and little else. Absence of endowment plus most houses are ill-constructed has caused the class of inmates to deteriorate so that many have to have parish relief to eke out existence. Pleased that anonymous gent invested £5,000 in Cannon Street ground rents and annual income given to Trust for £10 sustenance a year for as many aged persons as possible. Also recent improvement in income from resale of building land at Paul's Place and London Road should enable Trustees to make houses structurally more comfortable. The charity will be of much more public value. A few more benefactors would be welcome so that Trustees can raise all their old people above the necessity for Poor Law relief and so worthy old people hard hit in the battle of life may finish their days in peace and comparative comfort.'

Dover Municipal Charities

The Dover Almshouse Fund and a number of old Dover charities were merged into the Dover Municipal Charities during the 19th century. Included were the Gorely Almshouses, the James Neild Charity, the Jonathan Osborn Charity, the Coronation Pensions Charity, the Ann Booth and Mark Wills for Poor Widows Charity, the Gilham Gift, the Henry Matson Charity, the Hugesson's Charity, the George Crowhurst Rubie Pension Charity, the Needle Charity, the William Burchfield Charity. Dover's Battle of Britain Memorial Fund was added after the Second World War and the Grigg Christmas Boot Gift Charity in 1998. Details of some are given below.

Hugesson's Charity

By deed dated 20th September, 1633, James Hughesson gave £150 to the corporation, the interest to be applied at Michaelmas in every year, in 'placing forth two or three good male children' as apprentices. From 1701 £3 every year was distributed equally among six poor widows of Freemen. Each received this for life. The amount was paid for some years out of the Borough Fund to the Almshouse Charity Trustees. The reason for the alteration in the charity is unknown.

Ann Booth and Mark Wills Charity

Ann Booth in her will of 1664 gave £100 which was invested in land and the income of £13 5s. divided amongst six poor widows and Mark Wills in 1721 left certain lands with the profit to six poor widows each of whom received £2 a year.

James Neild Charity

Under a trust deed in 1810, James Neild transferred £800, 3% consols. The dividends were to be distributed in bread amongst, and in procuring the discharge of, debtors in Dover Castle Prison. When this prison was abolished the charity was merged with the Almshouse Charity.

Jonathan Osborn Charity

Jonathan Osborn, in his will of 1819, directed his executors to invest £100 in stock, and to divide the dividends among six poor men and six poor women.

Gorely Homes

In 1877 Mrs. Susan Gorely paid for ten almshouses to be built just below Cowgate Cemetery. The tenants were also given 3s. 6d. a week. She was the wife of Charles Gorely who had a farm in Ladywell. Park Street was laid out on part of the land in 1861. He died in 1874 and she in 1880. Dr. Astley who died aged 95 in 1907, left £14,000 to the Gorely Almshouses. Henry Hobday of Buckland Paper Mill provided further funds to extend the homes in 1921.

William Burchfield Charity

William Burchfield, by settlement in 1883, gave £2,000 consols. The income was to be paid to six 'decayed' i.e. impoverished tradesmen of Dover, elected by the corporation for life.

Battle of Britain Homes

The Battle of Britain Homes off York Street were funded from money originally raised to provide a new hospital for Dover possibly at Castlemount, but this never materialised with the arrival of the National Health Service in 1948. In 1955 the High Court ruled that the £34,000 collected could be used for some charitable purpose. Eventually it was decided to build almshouses to replace those which were to be demolished in York Street. The Battle of Britain Homes were built and the tenants of the York Street almshouses moved into them in 1964.

Gorely Homes in 2006

73

Battle of Britain Homes in 2006

Today the Municipal Charities of Dover own a substantial number of properties in the town, which produce income to maintain their modern 'almshouses' – not those of yore, most of which were destroyed during the Second World War – but the Battle of Britain Homes, Albany House, built in 1993 and the original Gorely Homes.

Other bequests for the benefit of the poor

There were many other bequests for the benefit of the poor, some of which survive to this day:

Thomas Pepper — four times Mayor of Dover, in his will of 1574 bequeathed an annuity of 40 shillings a year to be distributed equally between the parishes of St. Mary and Hougham. Originally the money was distributed as sixpenny loaves.

Thomas Ellwood — in 1604, gave 20s. yearly, for a distribution of bread.

Thomas Challice - in a 1613 bequest left 10s. a year for the poor.

Jacob Winser — in 1669 left the rents arising from eight dwellings near North Pier for the benefit of eight aged people plus 24s. a year for the poor.

Thomas White — in 1669 left 40s a year to give four poor widows 10s. each.

John Hewson — left £20 in 1692 with the interest to be spent on poor widows.

Nicholas Cullen   – in 1696, left a small dwelling in trust for bread for the poor; also 13s. each for 20 poor widows every New Year's Day. With an increase in income from 1781 the 20 poor widows each received a yearly sum of £6 10s.

William Richards   – in 1701, gave a rent charge of £5 to be distributed in bread.

Thomas Papillon   – a contractor for the navy, bought Acrise Place. He was a Puritan and essayist who contested one of Dover's two parliamentary seats when his religious views were out of favour. Charles II heavily supported his opponent to the extent of bribing the Town Council for its votes. However, Thomas won, but the Mayor declared his opponent the winner on a technicality. Thomas appealed, but his opponent was killed in a naval action and Thomas was appointed MP in 1673, serving the town for 22 years. Following an expensive lawsuit, which he lost and failed to pay the £10,000 damages, he retired to Holland. In his will of 1701 he left £400 'the profits from which were to be used to assist Freemen's sons under 25 to pay for their apprenticeship or setting up their own trade.' Any spare money could be used for the relief of the poor and aged in Dover. Applications for help are still invited and are considered by Dover Town Council.

Thomas Dawkes   – shipwright, in 1703, left £50 with the interest to be spent on bread distributed annually to the poor of St. James' Parish by the Minister, Churchwardens and Overseers.

Anthony Church   – left £20 in 1709 with the interest to be spent on bread for the poor.

Ann Jell   – in 1719, left a rent charge of 40 shillings a year to eight poor widows.

John Dekewer   – left £500 in 1760 with the interest to be spent keeping the tomb of Benjamin de Winke in repair. Any surplus was to be spent on bread and coals for the poor.

Thomas Beane   – by will dated 1764, left £200 in government stock and directed part of the dividends to be used for repairing the tomb of Jane Byron and Clement Buck at Old St. James' Church and the remainder spent on bread for the poor by the Minister, Churchwardens and Overseers of St. James's Parish.

Susanna Hammond – died in 1767 and bequeathed £60 with the interest to be used in a distribution of bread among the poor.

Elizabeth Roalf	– in 1777, left £12 a year to the 10 poorest families.
Thomas Knott	– in 1777 left a yearly sum of 20 shillings to 40 poor widows – 6d. each every St. Thomas's Day.
Thomas Boykett	– in 1791, left stock to yield £5 a year for the poor.
Peter Fector	– in 1806, bequeathed £200 of shares for relief of necessitous seamen and £100 with the interest to be divided among six aged widows.
Rebecca Sauce	– in 1808, bequeathed £400 3% consols with the dividends to be spent every two years repairing her husband's tomb and any surplus in the purchase of coals for the poor.
Thomas Pattenden	– the Dover diarist, died in 1817 leaving £850 3% stock with the dividends to repair the headstones of his family grave and to use the remainder among six poor widows, whose husbands had been drowned.
Lady Boothby	– died in 1822 and left her money to the poor of four parishes that she was acquainted with, including St. James' which received £477 in bank stock. Dividends were to be distributed to the poor at Christmas. She had visited Dover occasionally and lived here for a time and was buried in Old St. James' Churchyard. The Dover charity was founded in memory of her daughter, Penelope, who had died when six years old.
James Finch	– died in 1828, leaving £100 3% consols with the dividends to be given in bread. John Hammond gave £100 stock for the benefit of six poor widows to keep his monumental tablet in repair.
Sarah Rice	– in 1841, left £700 3% consols with the dividends to be paid to the Mayor and Senior Magistrate of Dover and spent on the purchase of coals for distribution at Christmas amongst 10 poor widows of Dover seamen.

Societies

From time to time, particularly during the 19th century, various townspeople came together either formally or informally to assist the less fortunate.

Dover Philanthropic Society

The Dover Philanthropic Society was founded in 1838 to distribute soup and bread to the poor and was based in Youden's Court off Market Street and carried on for at least six years. Its founder was a J. R. Williams who kept the Duchess of Kent eating house. Seeing unemployed, starving men in the Market Square, he discussed his concerns with Steriker Finnis, S. M. Latham and others. A fund was raised and the soup kitchen established.

Dover Needlework Society

The Dover Needlework Society was founded in 1851 to provide employment during the winter months and to sell the garments made at cost price.

Coals

Distribution of coal to the poor during winter was undertaken for many years by the Dover Benevolent Society in Caroline Place.

Burials

Help for the poor sometimes came in an unusual form. St. Mary's Vestry Meeting on 27 September 1849 agreed that ground at the eastern part of the New Cemetery (Cowgate Cemetery), sufficient for 1,000 burials, should be appropriated for the poor at a nominal fee.

Public concern

Extra help could also be spontaneous as a result of public concern. On 19 January 1850 the Dover Telegraph reported a public meeting held about relief for the unemployed poor. Due to unusually severe weather, many usual sources of work were not available resulting in vastly increased destitution, requiring extraordinary efforts to meet the need over and above the usual help with supplies of soup, coal, meat and bread. The Mayor called a well-attended meeting at the Old Town Hall to consider the best way to provide temporary relief. Revd. John Puckle, Vicar of St. Mary's, stated that many had called upon him for assistance, but he had no funds for the purpose. He said the meeting needed to decide how to raise a fund, the objects of it and how to administer it. He also suggested people should agree to donate so much a week during the severe weather to guarantee money was available, that any applicant should show that he was unemployed due to the severe weather and a committee be appointed, meeting every other day and making use of people with the best information about the applicants.

The Dover Anti-Mendicity Society

This was a local organisation, established in 1870, acting as a safeguard against beggars, which were apparently a great nuisance in the 19th century. Dover people could feel quite happy about sending them away empty-handed and 'there should be no hesitation in invariably refusing aid to beggars' who could be referred to the Mendicity Office. If they deserved relief, they would get it, apparently. The Dover Year Book of 1877 carried an annual report of the society of which Rev. P. Ward was the Hon. Sec. and Rev. F. A. Hammond, the Hon. Treasurer. The officer of the society, Mr. Wellard, had been appointed as master of the Dover Union Workhouse since the last report. Due to the economic depression and the large number of navvies in the neighbourhood, there had been a large increase in the number of vagrants admitted to the workhouse and convicted of crimes, mainly for begging and for being drunk and disorderly. The value of the society was demonstrated by comparing the number of tramps admitted to the workhouse in 1870-71 (2,732) with the number admitted in 1876-77 (more than a 1,000 less) and convictions were 129 compared with 33. Applications to the society, 169, had trebled since the previous year. This number was broken down into:

Tramps sent to their friends	15
Mechanics in search of work who had food and lodging provided	11
Tramps with bread and coffee and a ticket for the workhouse	26
Tramps with bread and coffee	33
Unworthy tramps i.e. who had money	23
Tramps who refused bread, coffee and a ticket to workhouse	7
Tramps with tickets for workhouse	39
Dover residents relieved by the Society	6
Dover residents referred to parish authorities	5
Enlisted	4

Sample cases were: a destitute family new to Dover seeking work with wife and two children suffering from measles – given help and sent to the workhouse next day; three destitute French people, a mother, son and paralysed daughter, were sent to Ostend; an unemployed man with wife and three children and fourth child who had recently died were supplied with food; an out of work man with a sick wife was given a loan of ten shillings which was repaid; but a woman, who claimed that her husband was ill and unable to work so that they and their children were destitute, was found to have no husband, had been living with a travelling chair mender for more than 10 years and had 3s. 6d. in her pocket!

Dover Charity Committee

Dover Charity Committee was instituted in 1906 supported by voluntary contributions. Its patron was Major Astor and the Mayor was chairman of the meetings in the Town Hall that were held every Thursday evening from November to May until 1939.

Orphanages

Dover Orphan Home for Girls

This home was situated at 98 Folkestone Road on the corner of Winchelsea Road and was established by the two Misses Haddon in 1865 with the object of providing a home for orphaned girls aged five and over who had lost either one or both parents and training them for domestic service. This was not for the destitute. Relations or friends of the girls were expected to pay a £5 entrance fee plus £2 10s. a quarter for maintenance with the rest of the cost borne by voluntary subscription. The two ladies ran the home until one of them died in 1891 when it was transferred to trustees and a committee of local gentlemen.

The *Dover Chronicle* of 11 May 1895 gave a detailed report of the annual meeting of subscribers and friends. Dr. Astley JP presided and amongst those present were Mr. Mummery, Mr. G. Chitty and Mr. Worsfold Mowll as well as a large number of interested ladies. Apparently there were 29 girls living in the home. The annual accounts showed £12 7s. 8d. in the bank but liabilities of £17 19s. 11d. It was agreed that more subscribers were needed but also more girls since they could be accommodated at no extra cost! There had been no illness of any sort in the past year. Mr. Osborne was the honorary surgeon, Revd. Dolman gave religious instruction every week, Miss Gill was the teacher and Miss Baker

Dover Orphan Home for Girls, 1933

Red-coated girls from the Dover Orphan Home for Girls, 1934

the matron. The children were taught to be practical servants and to understand housework, but Revd. Hugh Falloon, Vicar of Christ Church, commented, 'there was a great dislike these days of 'service' amongst young people who like to have their liberty, but it was the noblest work in which they could engage.' There were scholarships for domestic classes in the town and it was hoped to get cookery lessons for two girls. At the annual prizegiving Sir Richard Dickeson and Lady Dickeson were the guests of honour and prizes had been distributed for homework, needlework, school lessons, general conduct and conduct at school. Prizes took the form of 10 shillings deposited in the Post Office Savings Bank for the girls when they eventually left the home.

In 1934/5 the Trustees were J. H. Back JP, G. A. Bacon, Wilfred Chitty and Rutley Mowll. The Surgeon was Dr. C. Toland. Children attended Band of Hope classes and entered scripture examinations with considerable success. Money was raised by an annual flag day and by donations and bequests. Treats during the year were a garden party at Redstone, the home of Mrs. Rubie at Kearsney, the Christ Church Sunday School treat, the Temperance Garden fete at Coolderry, Temple Ewell, 12 girls went to a private Christmas party, 10 to a Priory School party and everybody went to a New Year party at St. James' Girl Guides. Two day trips to the seaside were provided by the committee.

Writing in 1993, Hubert Ashling recalled a visit to the home one Sunday in 1928 when he was four years old. He went with his father to visit his aunt, Gertrude Ashling, who was the matron of the home. Her youngest sister, Ivy, was the assistant matron. A Miss Harman was the school mistress and there was a cook and another lady. There were about 20 places. Very careful selection was made by the committee to ensure only healthy and presentable looking girls were accepted, for these girl were to become the servants of the gentry and the wealthy of the local area. The girls always appeared most happy and contented. They were well fed, clothed and educated above the average child. The furnishing and moral teachings of the large two storey Victorian house, remained back in mid-Victorian times. The girls were instructed in the teachings of the Church of England's interpretation of the Bible; of cleanliness being next to godliness and great play being made of the parables referring to the good and faithful servants to their masters.

After pressing the bell push, the heavy green door with its polished brass fittings was opened by one of the senior girls. She greeted the visitors by name with a broad smile, took their hats and coats and passed them to a younger girl. The girls always worked in pairs with the older experienced girl training the younger. Standing in the large reception hall everything looked spotless and highly polished. Wide stairs led to the first floor dormitories. The visitors were led to the private dining room and formally announced to Aunt Gertrude and the other ladies. Although father and son visited regularly, the girls always had to conduct themselves as though they were already in service. Everybody sat at the tea table and when Aunt Gertrude rang a small hand bell four girls glided into the room and served tea noiselessly and efficiently. When they had finished the aunt gave a signal and the girls cleared the table.

The aunt took Hubert from the room and down a familiar passage, passing the kitchen where the girls were washing up with much giggling and chatter, and into a classroom converted into a playroom. Dolls, prams and dolls houses were stacked around the walls, but the only toy the aunt knew Hubert was interested in was a rocking horse. Safely mounted, Aunt Gertrude left him to supervise the kitchen. Soon it was time to go and they left, carrying two pastries for Hubert's brother and sister.

Gordon Boys' Orphanage

Thomas Blackman, a local philanthropist, founded the Dover Youth Institute and later the Seaside Rest for boys living in London orphanages. This later became the Gordon Boys' Orphanage, which was opened in 1885 by the sister of General Gordon and named in his memory, following his death in Khartoum. The home took boys aged 9 to 16 who had lost one or both parents or who were destitute from all parts of the Empire. There was either no charge or a small payment of about a shilling a week. It occupied a large town house in St. James's Street, which was greatly enlarged over the years and eventually housed about 117 boys. The annual report for 1891/92 names the premises as Gordon House at 56 St. James's Street, Stewart House at 38 St. James's Street and the St. Martin's Upper and Lower School in Church Street. The staff consisted of the Upper School tutor, the Musical Director, Matron and Assistant, Lower School Tutor and Assistant and the Hon. Commandant, Thomas Blackman. Appeals were made for second hand clothing, bedding, carpeting and furniture as well as 'old linen for wounds.' New drums for the band and annual prizes were also needed and offers to knit socks were always welcome! The band had performed at Broadstairs

Gordon Boys with A.T. Blackman

81

Gordon Boys' Orphanage in St. James's Street

before Princess Louise and the Band of Mercy had reported cases of cruelty and kindness that its members had encountered. Much of the report was devoted to detailed lists of all gifts, both money and kind, received during the year, naming the donors and including all the stall holders at the annual bazaar. The Christmas dinner had also been donated. The accounts showed a deficit of £115 and an expenditure of £1,554. In 1912 its trustees were Sir William Crundall JP, H. Howard JP, A. T. Walmisley, R. E. Knocker the town clerk and Thomas Blackman who ran it with the aid of a management committee until the 1920s when a Mr. and Mrs. Stevens took over as master and matron. On Sunday the younger boys went to Old St. James' Church for a service whilst the older boys paraded to New St. James'. Full Scottish dress was worn on Sundays, but on weekdays the boys were rather meanly dressed in shorts and jerseys. They had to clean the premises both inside and out and had to do all the washing-up.

The rigid regime at the home was described between 1930 and 1940. There were two dormitories with 25 boys in each. The dormitories were scrubbed weekly by the boys and, if not thought clean enough, they did it again. There was

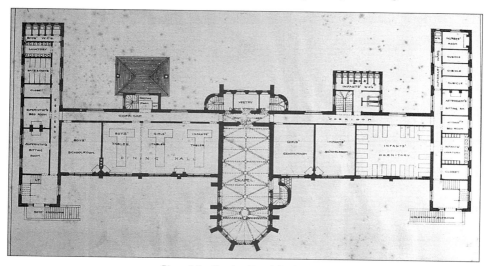

Plan of the Gordon Boys' Orphanage

a yard containing a shed where the boys washed. If dirt was found on the neck afterwards, a caning followed. There was porridge every morning with salt, not sugar. Tea comprised two slices of bread and jam, although there was a fairy cake on Sunday, if you were good. Boys who wet the bed had to sleep on boards; everybody was woken at 10pm and the bed wetters had to run out into the yard toilets in all weathers. Over the years the home supplied recruits to over 60 regiments as well as the Royal Navy. Some boys emigrated and some entered the professions. Dovorian Budge Adams said, 'Those of us who saw the boys daily gained the impression that their lives were not the happiest.' The home was badly damaged by shellfire during the Second World War and was demolished. The site would be at the rear of the County Hotel in Townwall Street.

The founder, Thomas Blackman, was born in Dover and his mother ran a preparatory school. Sunday School Superintendent of St. Mary's for 30 years, Thomas died in 1921, aged 74.

Home for Little Boys

A home for boys was established in 1892 at Barton House, Barton Farm for boys who had lost one or both parents and were too young for larger orphanages, but were in need of 'motherly care.' Other deserving cases were also eligible. It was not free. Relatives or friends had to pay £13 a year, monthly or quarterly in advance. If a parent remarried then the child had to be removed from the home. Upon admittance certificates of baptism and health were required plus a change of clothing and two pairs of boots. The boys attended Buckland School, but had chores to do in the home such as making their own beds, sweeping and dusting.

Barton Farm, Home for Little Boys

Visitors were allowed one afternoon a week, but friends and relatives could visit at any time. The home welcomed monetary donations as well as surplus clothing and toys. The annual report of 1898 mentions that due to a sudden collapse of a home in London eight little boys had had to be accommodated suddenly. By 1897 the home was at 22 Templar Street, having been forced to move from the farmhouse, which had to be demolished and by 1905 the home had moved again to Belmont in Priory Gate Road. The Honorary Superintendent was Miss Middleton and the Hon. Sec. Miss Munday. By 1912 the home had moved to 26 Templar Street and with the change of premises the 26 boys attended St. Bartholomew's schools. Dr. Koettlitz attended the sick. There was also a home for boys at 27 Pencester Road and in 1882 a home for waifs and strays in Biggin Street both managed by the Church of England.

Other Homes

Dover National Sailors' Home

This home was founded by Revd. William Yates, the priest of St. John Mariners' Church, in 1853 as a refuge for shipwrecked sailors. Several local ladies known to Yates guaranteed the cost of renting a home in Council House Street and providing a supervisor. In practice donations covered the costs anyway. When the long-established independent Cinque Ports' Pilots came under the control of Trinity House, funds which they controlled, namely Barque Money and Fector's Charity for Sailors, were transferred by the Charity Commissioners to the Dover Sailors' Home, enabling the building of a permanent home which cost over

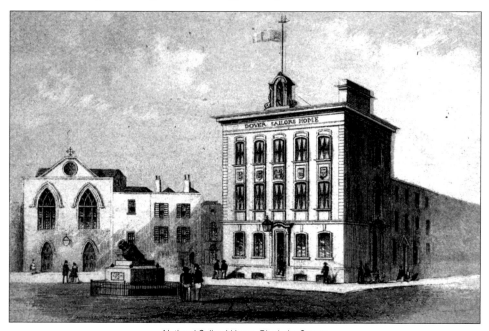

National Sailors' Home, Blenheim Square

£2,000. It opened in 1855 with 40 beds. The annual report for 1899 recorded that 1,160 men had slept there during the previous 12 months and 33,240 had attended the reading and recreation rooms. At that time there were a large number of distressed sailors attracted to Dover seeking work, but were unfit for the available labouring work associated with the building of the National Harbour. Forty men had received financial assistance. In 1906 14 shipwrecked crews totalling 132 men had been accommodated and 164 destitute seamen assisted. In addition 400 Royal Navy sailors had used the accommodation. The home was open daily except Sunday, although the reading and smoking rooms were open every day. There was a free lending library, weather reports were available and a marine barometer provided wind information. When the Dover Sailors' Home closed in 1923 its funds were transferred to the Dover Patrol Hostel in Wellesley Road on the corner with Liverpool Street. A similar home for soldiers existed in Castle Street.

Women's Hostels

The Home of the Good Shepherd run by Miss Hoare and supported by public description was in Market Street. By 1905 it was based in Prospect House in Princes Street open at all hours for the reception of any female 'desirous of leading a better life.' During the previous 17 years 700 women had been helped. In 1906 84 entered the home and 36 others were refused; ages ranged from 11 to 36 years. In 1912 there was a refuge for girls at 22 Templar Street and also a girls' hostel at 77 High Street managed by the Dover Preventive and Rescue Centre and run by Miss Quance. This hostel was still operating in 1948 at 2 De Burgh Hill.

Prospect House

R. V. Coleman Trust

Richard Vincent Coleman was born in East London in 1831 and purchased 'The Shrubbery' on Crabble Hill as his home in about 1843. When he died in 1909 he left property and shares for a charity to be set up. Subsequently, the R. V. Coleman Convalescent and Nursing Home Trust was established in 1914, based at The Shrubbery. The building was soon found to be unsuitable for the purpose and was demolished in 1923, but replaced with new premises on the same site in 1925. From 1938 it was used as a home for nurses working at the Royal Victoria Hospital and, following the Second World War when it was taken over by the military, was leased to the National Health Service. Terry Sutton recalls how he and his friends were invited into the nurses' home during the 1950s to 'entertain' the nurses, but had to leave by 9pm. The charity, however, still helps local people in need: the sick and disabled, the handicapped and infirm. In 1998 58 people were helped at a cost of over £25,000.

Dover Moral Welfare Association

Formed in 1896 to look after 'girls in trouble,' the Dover Moral Welfare Association moved its hostel in 1956 from 2 De Burgh Hill to St. Monica's in Folkestone Road, which had previously been the St. Martin's vicarage. It closed in 1968, reflecting the changing attitude to unmarried mothers.

St. Alphege Trust

Miss Kathleen George and Miss Anne Yarrow lived at 2 St. Alphege Road and in 1962 began to provide accommodation for immigrants passing through Dover, but they became aware of the great accommodation need of homeless girls and

St. Alphege Trust building

married women with children and in 1967 extended their hospitality to include them. The work was registered as a charity and the trust committee was representative of many local interests and reflected the support of most churches as well as the local authority and social services. When 1 St. Alphege Road was for sale it was purchased and rooms were converted into bedsits. Eventually 14 rooms were converted and the house was equipped with laundry facilities and a large common room. There were also two small rooms for one night emergencies. Residents stayed for short or longer periods until other satisfactory arrangements could be made. About 12 women and seven or eight children were accommodated at any one time. The home provided a haven where desperate women could relax and decide upon their future. In 1976 a large property at 22 Salisbury Road was also acquired and converted, providing two flats and a maisonette for longer term residents.

When Miss George and Miss Yarrow left Dover an Anglican order of nuns took over their role but in 1982 salaried warden and deputy were appointed. The charity was supported by local flag days, donations from Dover Carnival and other donations. It continued until the early 1990s when the properties were handed over to the Samuel Lewis Housing Trust, which rented them to the Marriage Guidance Council (later called Relate).

St. Martin's Emmaus

In 1994 there was still need for a night shelter in Dover for the homeless, although a greater need was somewhere for them to go during the day. Francis Watts, a local Christian, was instrumental in bringing the Emmaus Movement to the town to help meet this need. Begun by Abbé Pierre in Paris in 1949 the movement with over 400 communities worldwide provides a home, work and a

Archcliffe Fort, home of St. Martin's Emmaus

future for single homeless people. Every resident, or companion as each is called, must agree to respect other people, to refrain from bringing alcohol or illegal drugs into the community and to be available for up to 40 hours work each week. If a room is available it is open to anyone with no questions asked. A group of people representing local churches, businesses, the District Council and St. Martin's Trust, a local charity, supported the idea. The derelict Archcliffe Fort was identified as a suitable site and St. Martin's Emmaus was launched in 1995. The name was chosen to link it with the local charity and St. Martin, Dover's patron saint, renowned for dividing his cloak with a beggar. Kendal Beasley, a young nurse, was the first coordinator and the first 'customer' arrived on New Year's Eve. Most of the money was raised locally. The target, achieved as money became available, was to renovate buildings to house up to 21 companions each with their own en suite room and communal sitting and dining rooms plus a building to house, restore and sell donated furniture and other goods to enable the community to be self-supporting. Rosie Barnfather succeeded Kendal. By 2006 average sales were £3,000 a week. Companions sometimes just leave, but some leave to live and work locally, others stay at Emmaus for several years.

Soup kitchen

The 20th century welfare state, even supplemented by national and local charities, did not abolish homelessness and destitution. A modern 'soup kitchen' was launched in 1990 by Stephanie Perrow of River Methodist Church to help meet the needs of people sleeping rough by providing food and drink every evening. Several churches agreed to provide volunteers and food every day of the week. Initially it operated from the boots of cars, but eventually from a donated portakabin in Russell Street car park. The project is still much used in 2006 and involves some 200 volunteers, including some non-churchgoers. Customers vary in number from six to 26 each evening and include men, women and even teenagers, some of whom have drug or alcohol problems, some who years ago would have been in psychiatric hospitals and others unable to cope with the stresses of modern life. The service does not stop at Christmas. Festive dinners are provided on Christmas and Boxing Day by volunteers at a town centre church, attracting some 25 appreciative folk.

Chapter 8

EDUCATING THE POOR

In medieval times larger monasteries would have three types of school: a song school for the children, but no more than six, of the local well-to-do who would be taught to sing the psalms and to read; a school for novices and young monks little more than three in number taught by an older monk and prepared for monastic life; and grammar schools catering for no more than ten pupils destined to become clergymen or university students. There is a late 14th century reference to such a school at Dover Priory and a payment of £2 13s. 4d. recorded in 1535 as the yearly stipend of 'the grammar school master.' These local opportunities for the education of the rich disappeared with the Dissolution of the Monasteries, but over the succeeding centuries the rich have always made provision for the education of their children, particularly their sons, using boarding schools, private day schools or even private tutors.

Education of the poor was a different matter with no provision at all in Dover until the 17th century when, in 1616, the town council voted £8 a year to Revd. Robert Udney, curate of St. Mary's, to give free education to six poor children of the town. It was held in the old Court Hall in the Market Square with a chamber for the master's living quarters.

A few prominent individuals were also moved to help. In 1721 Henry Furness, MP for Dover, purchased two houses and founded a free school for boys. John Trevanion, who became an MP for Dover in 1774, established a school for 50 poor boys in Council House Street in the Pier District and supported it as long as he remained an MP – until 1803. According to Bavington-Jones in his Annals of Dover, an infant school was also started by the Minet banking family in the same area.

Later, leading townsmen provided a charity school in Queen Street with a house for the master and mistress, which was established in 1789.The school rules included 'This institution is designed to instruct 45 boys and 35 girls in the

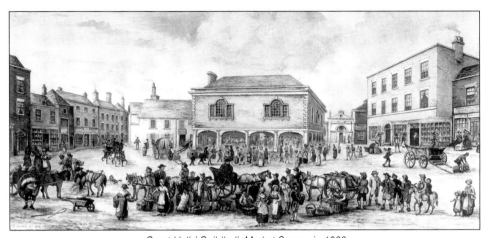

Court Hall / Guildhall, Market Square in 1822

St. Mary's (later National) School building in Queen Street

principles of the Christian religion, as it is taught in the established Church of England; in singing of plain psalm tunes …, in reading, writing and arithmetic. The girls to be further instructed in plain needlework and knitting …' Larger, purpose-built premises were provided in the same street in 1820. It had two lofty rooms for 200 boys and 200 girls and was supported by voluntary subscription and funds raised by annual sermons preached in several Dover churches. According to the memoirs of Mary Horsley, the pupils were supplied with headgear for church: girls wore tall black bonnets tied under the chin and boys wore black leather caps crossed with yellow braid. Government grants became available from 1862, although they were based on an infamous 'payment by results' scheme. No pupils were under eight years of age.

A school of industry was established in 1818 for the instruction of 60 girls under the direction of some ladies, which used a private house until 1827 when premises were obtained in Durham Hill. Ann Bailey, who was born in 1815, later recalled another school in Queen Street supported by the Quakers.

Ladywell Lane Boys' Ragged School

One of the great movements of Victorian philanthropy, the so-called ragged schools, provided for children and young people who were excluded by virtue of their poverty from other forms of schooling. They date back to about 1818 but didn't really increase substantially in number until the formation of the Ragged School Union under Lord Shaftesbury in 1844 when there were about 20 ragged schools countrywide. This number rose to over 600 by 1867. The Dover school was, however, never part of the Union. It is fortunate that records of this school from 1850 to 1854 were discovered at the bottom of the Worsfold family trunk when presented to the Dover Museum in 2000, making the following detail available.

The Ladywell Lane Ragged School opened on 1 January 1850. It was founded by the Dover Scripture Readers' Society for those 'sadly neglected children whose parents, through extreme poverty and, in many instances, through extreme depravity, are unable and unwilling to send them to the day schools already in existence'. The Society had proposed the formation of an evening school where 'instruction shall be chiefly religious ... and based strictly on the Word of God. The secular instruction should be elementary and perfectly simple'.

The Society promoted the idea of the school to its members and to the townspeople in general to raise subscriptions to fund it. The stated aim for the school was that 'the ignorant, vicious and degraded vagrant is reclaimed and changed into the industrious, useful and peaceable subject'. Underlying the general rise in Victorian philanthropy towards the working classes was a genuine belief that the dangerous elements of society could be brought into line through religion and education: 'For the ignorant and degraded ... the choice lies between preventive and remedial measures, between school or gaol, between scriptural education or the prison ... it is in the power of every townsman to determine whether that generation rising up around them shall be one of vagrants and vagabonds, of thieves and criminals, or of loyal subjects and useful citizens.' The school's role, as they saw it, was to 'combat ... the number of low and bad houses of various descriptions existing in this town, where drunkenness, profaneness, lewdness and immorality hold an almost undisturbed sway ... an evil which entails so much vice and misery upon the town.'

Ladywell Lane Boys' Ragged School

The Society negotiated with the Mayor, Steriker Finnis, for the free use of a redundant building for six months and was given a property in Ladywell, built over the river, next to what is now Dover Police Station. A similar Girls' Ragged School was founded off Adrian Street in 1851. A Superintendent, Edward Leach, was appointed to the boys' school at an annual salary of £8 16s. to be 'in charge of classes and school, to visit the parents and associated of the boys, seek out those who have not yet placed themselves within the school's influence.'

Costs for the first year of operation were £56 9s. of which £20 7s. 8d. was spent on repairs and alterations to premises. In addition £1 18s.6d was donated to pay for the Christmas dinner and £10 13s. for two treats. Income other than these donations was £49 2s. 6d. producing a loss of £7 6s. 6d.

All teaching and instruction was provided free by volunteers from the Society and the general public. These volunteer teachers included all Dover's leading philanthropists, including ex-mayors such as Michael Elwin (solicitor and magistrate) and Edward Poole (iron founder), town councillors and mayors-to-be such as Parker Ayers (builder), John Friend (importer), Edward Knocker (solicitor) and William Mummery (tanner). Other influential people included Thomas Fox (lawyer and clerk to the Dover Union), Thomas Ismay (ironmonger), Alfred Kingsford (brewer), Charles Lucus (Cinque Ports' Pilot) and George Shepherd (artist and photographer). However, the two men who were the driving force behind the school, as well as its senior officers, were Christopher Worsfold and William Mowll. Christopher Kilvington Worsfold was a founding member of both the Scripture Society and the Dover Benevolent Society. He had taken over from his father, James, the family firm of Worsfold & Hayward, auctioneers, surveyors, estate agents and accountants. He was also Chamberlain and Treasurer to Dover Corporation, Treasurer to the Urban Sanitary Authority, and Churchwarden of Christ Church in Folkestone Road. William Rutley Mowll JP was a coal merchant operating from Commercial Quay on Wellington Dock. He lived in a mansion on Biggin Street, later moving to Chaldercot in Leyburne Road, and became Chairman of the Dover Gas Company. Like Worsfold he was involved in a number of other good causes: President of the Dover Young Men's Christian Association and also the organising secretary of the Dover School Managers' Association which built several Dover schools including Granville Street Boys' School.

The ragged school opened every weekday evening from 6.30pm to 8.00pm with a Sunday school from 3pm-4pm. Later the school obtained permission to take smartly-dressed lads to Sunday service at St. Mary's 'for public worship ... with decency and propriety' and so also began a Sunday church meeting at 8.30am. Normal classes opened and closed with a prayer and short Bible lessons were read and explained. The Ten Commandments were repeated aloud and committed to memory. Portions of Scripture were also taught and a hymn sung every evening. Secular instruction consisted of spelling, reading, writing on slates and simple arithmetic. The teachers' arithmetic lessons book reveals 'simple' maths including multiplication and division of eight figure numbers, compound addition, subtraction and multiplication. A typical problem was 'A Factor bought 86 pieces of Stuff which cost him £517 19s. 4d. at 4s. 10d. per yard. I demand how many yards there were and how many ells English in a piece'. The volunteer teachers would often give special lectures, usually on a religious theme but also on their own hobbies and interests; for example Mr. Mowll gave lectures on astronomy while Mr. Mummery gave illustrated talks on animals, including a 'pleasing and instructive lecture upon the Oyster.'

The school register lists 198 boys in total and the school log reveals that in the first year daily attendance averaged about 100 boys in winter, 60 in summer and 30 on Sundays. Three or four teachers attended every evening. This is impressive, considering that the school encountered fierce opposition from some working class people. This was not just a reluctance to send their children to the school but a real fear that the children were in some way being 'stolen' and were certainly being removed as economic assets capable of bringing earnings to the family. This resulted in some quite serious vandalism to the school, including several attacks on the property whilst class was in session: 'the Committee had to encounter the difficulties and disagreeables which have beset nearly every similar enterprise. The windows were smashed, the lights blown out and the coarsest language was used – there was disturbance without and tumult within, … it has been necessary to secure the aid of the Police to shield the boys from the violence of their former comrades'.

The boys' ages ranged from six to one of 19 with the majority being between 10 and 15. On admission 45 were listed as able to read, 42 as able to read a little and 60 not able to read at all. Their addresses confirm that the boys were from the poorest areas of Dover with most coming from notorious slum areas such as Barwick's Alley, Spring Gardens, Paper Alley, Union Row, Fish Alley, Blucher Row and Dolphin Court. Most were from Charlton and St. Mary's parishes. The register, on occasion, also records a few extra details such as Richard Chadwin, aged 14, 'a fishing boy of Townwall Lane, totally ignorant' and Michael Hayes of the *Three Tuns* who 'obtains his living by begging.'

The school was forced to take into account some of the child labour needs of the local community. Numbers attending began to fall rapidly in July 1850 and on 5 August the decision was taken to close the school 'for 4 weeks in consequence of the Harvest.' School recommenced on 2 September, but attendance was still poor for the next two weeks until the 16th, when numbers suddenly rose 'due to brick-making being relinquished for the season.' Although it had initially been intended to open the school 365 days a year, from then on it was either closed or on reduced hours for most of the summer each year. As well as being forced to close during the periods of seasonal employment, the school closed more willingly for certain other days: on 19 November 1850 because the committee wished to attend the town meeting 'to address the Queen upon the Papal aggressions,' for the annual meeting of the Friends of the Boys' Ragged School each spring, the Girls' Ragged school annual meeting each winter and also for meetings of the Religious Tract Society. Other occasions included a concert evening for the Patriotic Fund, a failure in gas supply and a day 'set apart by the Nation for prayer and humiliation' on 26 April 1853.

To try and encourage attendance, surprise treats were given on a regular but unannounced basis. This was 'useful in attracting the boys, making them regular in attendance, and awakening in them gratitude and good humour.' The treats consisted of bread and cheese, gingerbread nuts, tea and buns, etc. When Sunday morning service was introduced a breakfast of a half-pint of coffee and a biscuit was served. On the odd occasion a treat was provided by some person of virtue such as that paid for by Lady Ford or the buns and gingerbread nuts paid for by the Revd. Tate and served to the 14 die-hards who turned up on 7 July. This was a reward 'in consideration of their absenting themselves from the Fair held this evening in Charlton Meadows.' A treat being served when temptations were at their highest became a regular feature, such as the annual Regatta Day or the passing of the Baltic Fleet, but attendance was still usually poor, only two turning up for Sunday School when the Fleet was passing. Sometimes, it seems, word of a treat must have got out such as when 120 boys received beef, cake and tea on Friday 20 October 1854, even though attendance during the few weeks previously had always been about 70 or 80 each day.

Christmas dinner was served at noon every Christmas Day as most working class homes would not have marked the day at all. Roast beef, potatoes and plum pudding were served and a gift of an orange made to every boy as he left. The poorest boys were issued tickets to ensure there was space for them at the dinner. Naturally this was one of the best attended days, a record 184 being present in 1853.

It was with some pride that the first visit by 'old boys' is recorded in the school log. Wood and Goldsack, then serving with the Royal Navy as First Class boys on HMS *Medea*, had attended the school from 1850. They returned in 1853 and their improved appearance was acclaimed as 'another instance of the usefulness of this establishment.'

The school started its own clothing fund in 1852 primarily to provide the children with 'Sunday Best' to allow them to attend church. This mostly paid for trousers and shirts, boots and shoes from local suppliers. Parents contributed a few pence each week to the fund until, with a contribution from the fund, the purchase price was reached and the item was handed over. For instance, Thomas Geddes needed a pair of trousers costing 8s. 6d. for which his parents made 15 payments of two or three pence a time from 1 March 1852, amounting to 5s. 8d. in total, the fund contributed 2s. 10d. and the trousers were purchased on 28 February 1853! On occasion the fund would buy clothes directly for some boys who had urgent needs and by the end of 1852 it was also helping out pupils at the Girls' Ragged School.

The Ragged School continued until 1871 when state education, following the 1870 Education Act, made it redundant. The last annual report, dated September 1870, was given by Worsfold, still Honorary Secretary & Treasurer. Mowll, Lucus, Kingsford, Mummery and many other founders were still listed as subscribers and teachers.

The building later became the Union Hall. Because it projected out into Ladywell it was partly demolished in the 1890s to set back its frontage and straighten and widen the road. It was totally demolished in 1938 with neighbouring buildings and replaced by the new police station and a garden adjoining the river.

Church schools

During the 19th century two societies were active in the country building church schools. The exclusively Anglican National Society for Promoting the Education of the Poor was founded in 1811 and built National Schools as they were known. It required children to be instructed in the Holy Scriptures and in the liturgy and catechism of the Established Church and to attend church services, teachers to be members of the Church of England, parish clergy to supervise the schools and inspections to be made by the society or the bishop. British Schools with no religious barriers followed and were built by the British and Foreign School Society, founded in 1814. The first government grant, of £20,000, was made to education in 1833, shared between the two societies. This was increased to £30,000 in 1839, followed by regular increases. With these grants came government appointed inspectors to supervise the schools receiving the grant. A British School was established on Finnis's Hill in 1834 and by 1847 it had 150 boys and 60 girls on roll and existed until 1885. Its annual report for 1877 reveals the extent of local voluntary effort required to keep the school going: a grant of £130 plus annual subscriptions of £41 meant an excess of expenditure over income of £131. This shortfall had to be made up from proceeds of jumble sales. A National School, Holy Trinity Infant School in Hawkesbury Street was built in 1839 for over £1,400 and St. John's, Blenheim Square in 1857 to serve the Pier District.

When voluntary schools were given government grants there was controversy over the degree of government supervision and religious instruction given particularly in Church of England schools; however, a compromise was reached in 1840 when school inspectors were accepted by the Anglican Church.

Several more church schools were established in the town over the next thirty years. The old Wesleyan Chapel in London Road was used as both a day school and a Sunday School after the new chapel opposite (now the King's Hall) was built in 1839, but only as a Sunday School once Buckland Church of England

St. James' School in St. James's Street

Holy Trinity School, Hawkesbury Street, rebuilt 1867, demolished 1963

Teachers of Holy Trinity School in the 1870s

School opened in 1842. This school was first housed in a wooden building on land which is now part of St. Andrews' Cemetery. It moved later to a more substantial building on the riverside below Buckland Bridge, but in 1860 the London Road premises were built for £1320 with the help of a government grant. Charlton School opened in 1841, Christ Church opened infants', girls' and boys' schools in 1847 on Military Hill and St. James' School in St. James's Street opened in 1848. Another Holy Trinity school in Round Tower Street opened in 1847 for older children. In 1858 the master's salary was £80 a year, the mistress's £48 and the infants' mistress £30. By 1867, however, this boys' and girls' school was in the way of the London, Chatham and Dover railway line and was demolished. Whilst the company built a replacement on a new site at the end of Hawkesbury Street, the school met for a year in the old Ship Hotel. The Roman Catholic Church opened a school in 1871, adjoining St. Paul's Church in Maison Dieu Road. In addition to these church schools J. Finnis & Son, the local timber company, erected school premises at East Cliff in 1846 and maintained them for 50 girls and a considerable number of boys who were taught for 2d. a week each.

In 1870 the Queen Street Charity School became a National (Church of England) school, named after and managed by St. Mary's Church. Another building was provided in Princes Street in the following year to house the girls, leaving the original building for the boys. An infants' school that had first opened in 1826, using a house, later moved to St. Mary's Mission Hall in Adrian Street and then moved into part of the new girls' school in Princes Street.

The rapid increase in the number of schools in Dover during this period demonstrates the growing belief that education was the key to lifting children out of poverty, although the voluntary providers could not afford to make it completely free.

1870 Education Act

The Education Act of 1870 marked the end of the total reliance upon charity or church schools for poorer people who could afford only minimal fees. The responsibility of the state moved from a merely supervisory role to more direct intervention. It was a landmark, introducing state provided schools where necessary to supplement local voluntary effort in order to ensure that all children received an elementary education.

The government contributed two thirds of the maintenance costs of new schools with the remainder coming from town rates levied by locally elected school boards. The levy could not be used to assist voluntary schools. These school boards had discretionary powers to enforce the attendance of children to the age of 13. School attendance for 5 to 10 year olds became compulsory in 1880. Children leaving school aged 10 could work, provided they had reached a certain educational standard. These new state or 'board' schools charged fees of a few pence a week, but poorer children were excused payment.

In Dover the Dover School Managers Association was formed to avoid having a local school board, thereby maintaining the voluntary principle. Voluntary schools continued receiving substantial grants, but the drawback was that government grants were capped and the difference had to be made up with public subscriptions and fees. Later, in 1891, the government introduced a grant of 10 shillings a pupil to all schools, enabling them to cease charging fees.

Controversy surrounded the 1870 Act. The right to withdraw any child from religious instruction on grounds of conscience was guaranteed. Local churchmen were incensed at the requirement not to teach any particular creed or catechism and local ratepayers demanded in vain that they should be represented on the management of church schools.

The Act resulted in a rapid increase in the number of elementary schools nationally. Between 1870 and 1876 there were 1600 building grant applications nationally with two thirds of the one and a half million new school places provided by the voluntary sector rather than local authorities. The Act did nothing about secondary education, which was restricted to public schools and endowed/voluntary fee-paying grammar schools.

To meet the target set by the 1870 Act Dover had to find extra school places for 568 older children and 712 infants. The Dover School Managers Association decided to meet the target by building the Granville Street Boys' School at Charlton in 1875, whose chairman was Canon Puckle of St. Mary's, and 390 infants' places would be created at Tower Hamlets, the Pier District and Charlton. St. Bartholomew's boys' school was built in Widred Road in Tower Hamlets in 1881. St. Bartholomew's Mission House in Black Horse Lane, later renamed Tower Hamlets Road, served as both a church and girls' school.

According to Kelly's Dover Guide of 1882, Dover's non-private schools then accommodated 4,766 children:

	Boys	Girls	Infants	Total
Christ Church National School Military Hill	157	134	101	392
Charlton National School	200	200	200	600
Dover National School Queen Street	454	265	265	984
Holy Trinity National School				430
St. Andrews Buckland	200	200	160	560
St. Bartholomew's School Widred Road	210	190	200	600
St. James' National School	200	161	136	497
St. John's Blenheim Square				100
St. Mary's Infants, Chapel Place				100
British School, Finnis's Hill				350
St. Paul's Catholic School				153

Barton Boys' School was built on Barton Meadow in 1898 by Buckland Parish, followed by an infants' school in 1902. The St. Martin's Schools for 700 infants, boys and girls were built in Markland Road in 1903. The Barton Road Schools, managed by Buckland Church, were soon in financial difficulties and were taken over by the town at a cost of £8,922 in 1904. To bring some existing schools up to standard the Whitehall Board of Education, established in 1899, ordered alterations to Holy Trinity School, St. James' Girls' School and St. James' Infants' School as well as more accommodation at River.

Thus, by the turn of the century elementary education was available for all the children of Dover, no matter how poor, whilst richer families could make use of the many small private schools in the town.

Granville Street Boys' School, 1888

Belgrave Road Infants' School, 1925

St. Martin's School in the 1930s

1902 Education Act

Following the 1902 Education Act, a Dover Municipal Education Committee was established responsible for elementary education up to 13. County councils took over responsibility for secondary education e.g. county (grammar) schools, which were fee-paying. In 1907 the government required all secondary schools receiving grants from local education authorities to reserve 25 to 40% of free places for children from elementary schools. In the same year a schools' medical service began. By 1912 there were 6,444 pupils in Dover's elementary schools of

Buckland School Infants 1907

Christ Church Girls' School c.1905

Boys of St. James' School including Gordon Boys c.1910

Charlton Girls 'on parade' c.1910

whom 4,272 were in denominational schools and 2,172 in town council schools. The Act also provided for the support of voluntary schools from local rates as well as government grants.

The Act meant that the county took over the Dover Municipal School, which shared premises in Ladywell with the Dover School of Arts and Sciences. In 1905 the school became the Dover County School for Boys and Girls. Fees were about five guineas a term but there were some scholarships. In 1910 the girls moved to separate premises in The Paddock.

In 1907 the town council was concerned about the ever increasing cost of education, including teachers' salaries and the government's demands for more school places. Costs had increased by £5,000 a year since the 1902 Education Act. During 1907 the council had to purchase St. Martin's School for £6,750 and then expand it.

Possibly Empire Day at Buckland School, early 1900s

County Girls' School, The Paddock, 1905

Kent County Council announced that a new building for the County School for Boys was to be built on Frith Road, which opened in 1915. It was only nine years later that it was decided to replace the Frith Road premises with another new building off Astor Avenue. It was expected to cost £50,000. Ten acres of land were donated by Mr. Leney, the Dover brewer, for playing fields and the new school was opened by the Duke of Kent in 1931.

The building of two other new schools began in 1911, a council infants' school at the Pier in Archcliffe Road and a girls' school at Barton Road. The town council took over the Christ Church Girls' School in 1914.

County Boys' School

Pier Infants' School, Archcliffe Road, 1936

Between the Wars

The First World War meant a loss of teachers for war service. The 1918 Education Act raised the school leaving age to 14 and abolished any remaining fees for elementary education. Any school accommodation problem was solved temporarily by the reduction in population. In 1922 there were 1,000 fewer children than in 1914. Staff reductions were resolved by dispensing with married women teachers as far as possible. There was no Equal Opportunities Act then! The nutrition of poor children was helped considerably by the government's introduction in 1921 of free milk for school children in need.

The following example shows what had become possible for poor children with government support in the interwar and later periods. Lillian Kay, born in

Girls of St. Martin's School c.1923

Astor Primary 1929

Boys of Barton Road c.1924. Joe Harman is in the front row, 5th from the left

poor circumstances in the Pier District in 1914, left Pier Infants' School, aged 7, to go to Holy Trinity school for 'big boys and girls.' Boys were on the ground floor with four classes in one large room and a small classroom for children staying beyond standard 4. This arrangement was repeated upstairs for the girls. On her first day Lillian spotted a notice in the cloakroom announcing 'Scholarships available.' Thinking that this was probably something worth having, she asked her mother for one. Mother told the head teacher who said that Lillian would have to wait until she was eleven. She did and Lillian was the first child from the school to win a scholarship to the County School and completed her own teaching career as headmistress of the same school, renamed Dover Grammar School for Girls!

The local committee in 1925 considered new schools to replace those church schools condemned by the Board of Education, namely Christ Church School for Girls, St. James' Infants and Buckland Infants. A new school to accommodate 400 children was also needed for the new houses off Astor Avenue. The Board of Education also wanted St. James' Boys' School closed in 1927 and was not happy with Buckland Infants' and the Roman Catholic school. Christ Church Girls' and Infants' remained open awaiting a replacement. They closed in 1929 when staff and pupils transferred to the new school, Astor Avenue Girls' and Infants' School. Ten years later it was restricted to over 11s.

Reorganisation

In 1926 the Hadow report, produced for the government, recommended organising elementary schools into those for under 11 years (with infants and juniors), called primary, and for those over 11, called secondary. Dover drew up its plans in 1928, including the need for five new schools. Building of the Astor Avenue school for under 11s began and it opened in 1929. Details of the

St. Bartholomew's Infants Class 2 in 1931

reorganisation were announced in 1931. Unfortunately, these elaborate plans were suspended due to the economic depression of the early thirties.

The reorganisation plans were resurrected and revised in 1935. If implemented, the transition would have been very disruptive. North Dover was to be served by a new school for senior boys (11-14) on the Shatterlocks allotment site, whilst senior girls would still be based at Barton Road but with two more classrooms. The rest of Barton Road Boys would be for junior boys only and both Buckland and Charlton would only take junior girls. Charlton's infants would move to Barton Road Infants whilst Buckland's infants would move to a new school at St. Radigunds. South Dover containing St. Mary's, Holy Trinity, Christ Church, St. Paul's R. C., St. James' and Pier Infants' schools were also affected. St. James' Boys', Girls' and Infants' Schools would be for senior girls only; its senior boys would move to St. Mary's in Queen Street and junior boys to Christ Church. Junior girls would move to St. Mary's Girls' School in Princes Street, which would lose its senior girls. A new St. James' Infants was planned for 150 pupils. The Roman Catholic Church opposed plans to move its senior boys and girls and junior girls to other schools. West Dover would have a new senior boys' school for 360 in Astor Avenue, taking boys from St. Martin's, Christ Church and St. Bartholomew's. St. Martin's would only have juniors. Astor Avenue Girls' School would be enlarged and used by senior girls only. St. Bartholomew's Boys' School would be for junior boys only and its girls' and infants' schools would be for junior girls only. Astor Avenue would have a new infants' school for 250 absorbing St. Bartholomew's infants. The total number of school places would be 6,585.

The County School for Girls with over 300 pupils moved into the vacated but enlarged Frith Road premises of the County School for Boys in 1935, enabling the School of Art, which shared the Technical School premises in Ladywell to move into The Paddock premises in 1938. Kent Education Committee planned a new technical institute off Astor Avenue, which was never built.

St. James' School 1929

Boys of St. Martin's School, Class 3 c.1926

Reorganisation of the town's elementary schools made some progress with a new infants' school planned at St. Radigunds, a senior school at Shatterlocks and Buckland church schools to be a junior girls' school. Rebuilding of the Roman Catholic school next to St. Paul's Church was also planned. In 1937, however, the plans were revised again with two areas for senior schools: Shatterlock Boys' for 480 with another at Astor Avenue. Up to 480 senior girls would be housed at an enlarged Barton Road school and Astor Avenue Girls' was to be enlarged to accommodate 480. St. Mary's Boys' would be for juniors only and St. James' would be a junior school only. Even this plan was thrown into doubt when it was suggested later that St. Mary's and St. James' should be retained for senior boys and girls. No decision was reached! St. James' Boys' School was, however, closed in 1938 with still no decision about St. Mary's Boys.'

The Board of Education lost patience with the long delayed reorganisation of Dover's elementary schools and issued an ultimatum in 1939 that Dover would lose the government grant of £85,000, 50% of the cost, if the latest scheme were not completed by 1940. The plans were quickly adopted with two new senior boys' schools at Shatterlocks and Astor Avenue and not using St. Mary's. With the outbreak of war, however, all new school building was postponed except for St. Radigund's Infants' which was under construction.

Second World War

By June 1940 all Dover schools were closed with pupils and staff evacuated to South Wales. The church managers of Holy Trinity School decided to close it permanently, but the local education committee decided to retain it as Dover Trinity School. Evacuation was voluntary and many children stayed in Dover, but no education was provided. With the end of the Battle of Britain children started to drift back to the town from Wales and in 1941 the Board of Education demanded the reopening of local elementary schools to provide part-time education. The town council preferred compulsory evacuation because of the continuing danger from cross Channel shelling and bombing, but the schools reopened in October, although attendance was not compulsory and only half the 1,200 children in Dover went. Consequently, the Board of Education urged full-time schooling, but the town council thought that this would encourage more children to return from Wales. Nevertheless, compulsory full-time education was introduced with some schools open: Pier Council School, St. Mary's in Princes Street, Christ Church in Military Road and Belgrave Road, St. Martins in Astor Avenue, St. Bartholomew's in Widred Road and Tower Hamlets, Barton Road, Buckland, St. Radigunds and River. By November 1941 there were 1,687 on local elementary school rolls and 574 in Wales. The two county schools, however, did not reopen in Dover until the end of the war.

1944 Education Act

The 1944 Education Act set the structure for post-war education and included the transfer of control of elementary education from boroughs to county authorities to which the town council took strong exception. It also raised the minimum school leaving age to 15, although it was not implemented until 1947, and in the state-maintained sector provided for universal free secondary education in three different types of school: grammar, technical and secondary modern in an attempt to cater for the different academic levels and aptitudes of pupils. Dover never gained a technical school and suitable pupils had to travel to Canterbury or Folkestone. Selection for grammar school was usually by an 11-plus examination. Church schools became part of the state-maintained sector whilst retaining their religious affiliations.

At the same time the school meals service was introduced available to all children, rather than the optional powers that education authorities had had since 1906 to provide cheap school meals to 'deserving' pupils in state elementary schools.

With this Act the long process of providing free education for all children up to school leaving age was completed, including free access to a grammar school rather than able but poor children having to rely upon winning scholarships to such fee-paying schools.

Post Second World War

In addition to implementing the 1944 Act, Dover had to prepare for the consequences of the post-war baby boom!

There were considerable changes in primary schools during this period. A new infants' school was built at Shatterlocks in 1948 and Powell Primary School, serving the Buckland Estate opened in 1949. This was supplemented by Melbourne Primary in 1954. Aycliffe Primary was built in the 1960s to serve the new estate behind Shakespeare Cliff, allowing the old Pier Infants' School to close, but the premises were used to house the Harbour School for special needs until it moved to new buildings at Elms Vale in 1977. The Roman Catholic junior school attached to St. Paul's Church was replaced by St. Richards in Castle Avenue in the late 1960s, using the buildings of St. Ursula's Convent School which had closed. St. Mary's Primary in Ashen Tree Lane opened in 1969 before the old Queen Street schools were demolished as part of the York Street redevelopment. Buckland School in London Road closed in 1969. St. Bartholmew's Infants' in Widred Road closed in 1977. Its pupils transferred to an

Castlemount in 1874

enlarged Astor junior school, which became Astor Primary. Vale View Primary also opened in 1977, allowing the old Belgrave Road junior school to close.

After the war the new secondary modern schools in Dover used Barton Road and Astor Girls' schools initially plus Castlemount, previously a private preparatory school, which opened in 1948. Astor Secondary School moved to new premises in 1951, leaving its old premises as a primary school. Archer's Court opened in 1957 as another secondary modern, allowing Barton Road to become a junior school. St. Edmund's, a Roman Catholic secondary modern, serving not only Dover but an area from Sandwich to Hythe, opened in 1962 with 360 pupils. Whilst the secondary modern schools were mixed, the two grammar schools remained single sex.

The 1960s brought arguments over the reform of secondary education with the Labour government's desire for wide ability comprehensive schools to replace secondary modern, technical and grammar schools. Headteachers and the local education authority debated how to implement the reforms without any new buildings. Various schemes were considered, but eventually, with a change of government, comprehensives were introduced, but grammar schools in Kent survived. The school-leaving age was raised to 16 in 1973 and in that year most of Castlemount was gutted by fire, but was rebuilt in 1977. This was shortlived as it closed in 1991. During the 1990s Astor Secondary was accommodated on one site and its premises on the other side of Astor Avenue were occupied by Astor Primary, which became Priory Fields School. By 2006 all Dover's secondary schools had either achieved or were seeking special school status in subjects such as the visual arts, the performing arts, computing, business studies and history.

Having begun this account of educating Dover's poor with no provision of any kind until a small beginning in 1616, it ends with every child at school until the age of 16 and most staying in education until 18 and all free of charge. Despite a general improvement in educational standards, however, 70% of children in receipt of free school meals – one of the deprivation indicators – still do not achieve the government's aim of 5 GCSE passes at grades A to C that is seen as necessary not only for social equality but also essential if Britain is to compete successfully in the global economy. This explains why 'Education, education, education,' to quote Prime Minister Tony Blair, is top of the political agenda today.

Chapter 9

UNEMPLOYMENT RELIEF AND HOUSING

In the 20th century both the government and the town council intervened far more than previously to improve the condition of the poor. Surprisingly, in 1904 the customary mayor's banquet, following the election as mayor for the 12th time of William Crundall, was not held due to the distress prevalent in the town owing to unemployment. Money that would have been spent by the council was given to a relief fund instead.

Work schemes to relieve unemployment

From time to time the town council devised work schemes or brought forward planned works in order to relieve unemployment, such as the extension of the tram service to River, which opened in 1905 and work on the Crabble Athletic Ground which the council had purchased. In 1923 as many as 16 schemes were considered, costing half a million pounds. Completion of the cliff road from the seafront to St. Margaret's attracted no grant from government and was dropped, but the widening of London Road at the foot of Crabble Hill, including the widening of Buckland Bridge was approved. These schemes were not, however, put into effect for many years. There were 1,400 unemployed in 1923, mostly unskilled ex-servicemen, but there was a shortage of skilled labour especially in the building trades. This was so acute that work at Dover Castle converting quarters for the additional fourth battalion was not possible.

More schemes were proposed in 1924, including the widening of the Folkestone to Dover road to the borough boundary, but Folkestone council was

Crabble Athletic Ground c.1897

against it. Building a football ground at Crabble for £23,000 was vetoed on cost grounds. There were plans for a football ground at Elms Vale and to extend main drainage to the rest of River. A proposal to make soccer grounds at Astor Avenue and Crabble was also rejected by the town council in 1925 when it took the view that it was the government's responsibility to relieve unemployment, especially when there was no benefit to Dover.

With the world-wide economic depression of the twenties and thirties the number unemployed in 1930 rose from 1,000 to 1,500. The town council relieved the situation by agreeing to supply free milk for school children of the unemployed and by providing some extra work, including building a football ground and children's play area at Crabble for £10,000. A new fire station in Ladywell was also agreed. These measures were followed by others in 1931 and 1932: a car park and small children's play area for Connaught Park, paths at Bunker's Hill and Shakespeare Cliff, a new mortuary in Hawkesbury Street and the enlargement of the museum and market hall. The construction of a high level water reservoir began, but was not completed until 1939, and the Union Road sewer scheme was proposed as well as the laying out of Lewisham Road, River, and new electricity showrooms and offices in Ladywell, which opened in 1934. Perhaps these efforts contributed to an improvement in the situation because at the first meeting of the Dover Employment Committee in December 1933, it was

Opening of the Dinners for Schoolchildren scheme,1933

Lady Violet Astor opening the Social Services Centre at the old Empire, 1933

Soup kitchen in the Town Hall, 1937

Old Folks' annual dinner, 1937

reported that there were 1,367 men and 124 women unemployed compared with 2,411 and 213 previous year. By the end of 1934 the unemployed total was fortunately down to 1,308.

In January 1933 Mayor Morecroft organised a soup kitchen, providing 1,500 dinners a week to needy children. Joe Harman remembered when, as a tram conductor, he would collect cauldrons of soup from the kitchens below the Connaught Hall in Ladywell and take them on the tram to the Pier schools. In the same year the Social Service Centre opened for the unemployed at the old Empire Music Hall and was attended by up to 500 a day from January until the summer when it closed. Despite the improvement in employment, special measures were still necessary to assist the poor. During the winter months of

1934 the Mayor again opened a successful soup kitchen by public subscription with over £174 raised. 18,584 'dinners' were given to children at a cost of less than 3d a head. The soup kitchen scheme was repeated in 1935 and a flag day raised £246. A similar flag day for the annual old people's dinner raised £177 in the same year.

In 1934 the Dover Unemployed Association held a carnival procession and fete in Pencester Gardens, raising £218 but only £70 after expenses were paid. This was distributed to the Gordon Boys' Orphanage, the Girls' Orphan Home, the Lifeboat Fund and 50% to the Dover Unemployed Association.

Once again the town council agreed to supply free milk to 484 needy school children in 1935. In the same year the Dover Work Training Centre became redundant following the establishment by KCC of Junior Instruction Centres at the School of Art and the Technical Institute in the old Northampton Street drill hall. Over the previous nine years the Centre had trained 650 boys with 80% obtaining jobs. Major Astor had personally contributed £7,667 toward the cost over this period. A new Unemployment Relief Act introduced new scales of payment which were sometimes lower than before, resulting in protests in Dover and elsewhere about the hardship caused. Subsequently, a deputation of the unemployed met the Board of Guardians Committee and this was followed by a meeting at the town hall. Later, the government was forced to guarantee the former levels of benefit and to introduce the reforms gradually. A sign of the times in 1935 was the gesture made by the French President, Monsieur Lebrun, when he handed £56 to the Mayor for the poor of Dover when returning to France after a visit to London.

Slum clearance and rehousing

By the beginning of the 20th century many of the back to back squalid houses packed into the streets of the Pier District and the Durham Hill area were

Beach Street

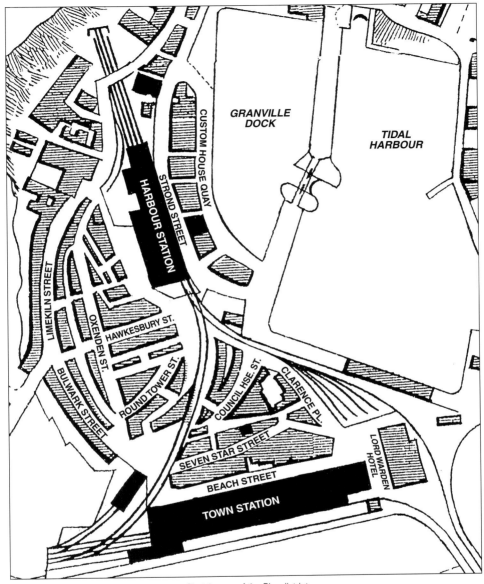

Sketch map of the Pier district

considered to be no longer fit to live in. Slum clearance began before the First World War. Following an inquiry in 1910 entitled 'Housing the Working Classes at the Pier,' the Local Government Board forced the council to demolish some Pier houses and to erect new replacements. The 1911 Dover Corporation Bill gave the council powers to borrow money in order to purchase dwellings compulsorily in the Pier District and to improve the road system there. It was planned to widen Limekiln Street, Bulwark Street and Great Street, reconstruct Beach Street, provide a new street to connect Beach Street with Seven Star Street

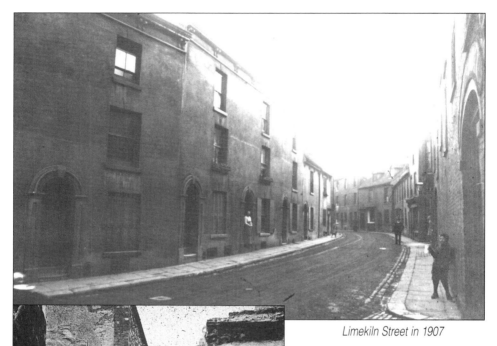

Limekiln Street in 1907

as well as a new sewage pumping station and outfall. At a Common Hall, a public meeting, held on 16 January 1912, the plans were rejected by a large majority, including probably many of the Pier residents affected. The council responded by balloting all ratepayers and won the ballot by 2,387 to 1,706, although half of those eligible declined to vote. The bill went through parliament but the Local Government Board included a condition that all the Pier people displaced over the previous 15 years should be rehoused. Consequently the council restricted its scheme to a modified viaduct and spur and the widening of Limekiln and Bulwark streets. Only 113 new houses would replace 311 to be demolished! Nothing was

Between Oxenden Street and Round Tower Street 1910

Oxenden Street 1911

Bulwark Lane 1912

Seven Star Street c.1912

The 1922 Viaduct

actually done until 1913 when the controlling Conservatives realised that they had to act before losing control of the council. Contracts were, therefore, awarded for the viaduct. In the meantime the Local Government Board had reduced its new houses requirement to 90 instead of three times that number. Nevertheless, the scheme was only carried by the mayor's casting vote. Work did start on the Beach Street end of the viaduct but with the outbreak of the First World War all work was suspended.

Albany Cottages, Adrian Row c.1936

After the war the council produced a scheme to clear slums in the town and to build 1,008 new houses, including 600 on the slopes of Old Park, what we now call the Buckland Estate, At the same time the Ministry of Health, that had succeeded the Local Government Board, decided that no new houses should be erected in the Pier District, but instead should be built on high ground overlooking Shakespeare Beach known as Ropewalk Meadow. Dover's contribution to the cost of this scheme was capped at a penny rate. The Pier scheme was resumed with the construction of a new Limekiln Street bridge, paving of the viaduct and demolition of the south sides of Limekiln Street and Bulwark Street as soon as new houses were

Adrian Street, 1935

Sketch map of the
Durham Hill area

available. In 1921 the Buckland housing scheme was reduced to 200 dwellings. They were not popular because the rates and rents were too expensive, particularly at a time when wages were falling. Extra private accommodation was being provided by some of the larger houses being converted into flats, including some in Waterloo Crescent. By 1922 the Pier viaduct was opened to traffic at long last and the Limekiln Street bridge contract was awarded and work commenced, making the new viaduct temporarily unusable!

The Buckland Estate houses were completed in 1922 and those at the Ropewalk in 1923, which were then occupied by Pier people. This was followed by the demolition of one side of the Limekiln and Bulwark streets. Oxenden Street was cleared during the same year and the council decided to demolish Seven Star Street, Blenheim Square, Finnis's Hill and the north side of Limekiln Street.

Durham Hill area

Further slum clearance was planned by the council in 1924 – Adrian Street, Mount Pleasant and the Seven Star Street area. The council decided 200 to 300 new small houses were needed.

There was uproar in the town in 1924 when the council proceeded with a parliamentary bill seeking an extension of time to complete the Pier scheme without the approval of a Common Hall meeting. The ratepayers called a meeting at which members objected to the bill. The Ministry of Health settled the matter by refusing to allow the council to proceed! With no empty houses and much overcrowding in 1924, the council devised ambitious building schemes, including 200 houses in the Astor Avenue area, although only 20 in total were built.

More council homes were

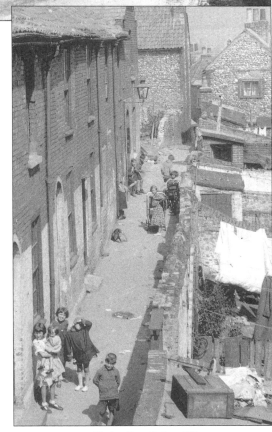

Blucher Row, Durham Hill
– houses declared unfit in the 1930s and demolished

built in 1925 in Tower Hamlets at Astor Avenue and Edred Road as well as at Shrubbery Cottages near Dodds Lane. More land was acquired north of the Boys' County School for another 200 council houses. Whilst another 30 council houses were built in 1927 at Noah's Ark farm at £541 per house, no further council housing schemes were recommended because of cost, despite demand. All the existing housing schemes were completed by 1928.

The1930 Housing Act, however, required a 5 year slum clearance plan. This was submitted to the Ministry of Health in 1933 and involved the demolition of over 300 properties and the rehousing of 1,400 people in 355 new homes:

1934   Seven Star Street area, Finnis's Hill, St. John's Place and Chapel Court – 58 houses.
1935   Adrian Street, Mill Lane, Chapel Cottages – 87 houses to replace 93.
1936   Pleasant Row, Queen's Court, Stembrook – 62 to replace 66 houses.
1937   Woolcomber Street area – 53 to be demolished, 64 improved and 91 new.
1938   Hartley Street area – 30 to be demolished, 25 improved and 35 new houses.

During 1932 30 houses at Buckland Estate were finished.

Durham Hill, scheduled for clearance in 1932, was not cleared until 1934 when 98 new houses at St. Radigunds were ready. Blucher Row and Mount Pleasant were also cleared. The disused Sailors' Home in Blenheim Square and the derelict mineral water factory were included in the same slum clearance orders. The planned clearance in the Pier would complete the removal of all the old property between the viaduct and Bulwark Street, which was started in 1913! Rehousing was to be in four blocks containing 36 flats in Limekiln Street plus a block of 28 flats in Seven Star Street.

The Limekiln Street flats were completed in 1935 and a start was made on 110 houses at the end of Union Road at the same time. A completely new layout was planned for the whole area at the foot of the Western Heights. The 1935 Housing Act required all Dover's dwellings to be inspected for any overcrowding and the building of council houses to remedy it. The outcome in 1936 was that out of 10,553 dwellings only 113 were considered to be overcrowded. The council, however, decided not to build the 41 new houses required because of the number of vacant properties available.

The Sailors' Home was demolished in 1936 and the town council decided to build another 36 houses and two shops in Union Road. Another three day fund raising carnival was organised by the Dover Unemployed Association.

The Adrian Street area was demolished during 1937 and 1938 with occupants rehoused at St. Radigunds or in new flats at the Pier. St. Mary's Mission Hall in Adrian Street was one of the casualties of demolition with the site being used for 12 cottages and a block of 6 flats. Adrian Street was to have 12 new houses and nine flats in three blocks. Completion of the clearance of the Durham Hill area was ordered by the Ministry. Chapel Court, off Snargate Street, and St. John's Place, next to the Grand Shaft, were also demolished. Market Court, Youden's Court and Mill Lane also went. The town council compulsorily purchased properties in Woolcomber and Trevanion Streets for further slum clearance.

Union Row prior to demolition in 1937

With the dramatic events leading up to the outbreak of war in 1939 council house building at St. Radigunds continued; houses started were completed but no new buildings were begun once war was declared. Similarly, slum clearance in the Durham Hill area continued and 66 houses in Stembrook were approved for demolition, but here too everything was suspended once war was declared.

Not surprisingly, therefore, at the end of the Second World War the most important problem facing the town was housing. Many homes had been destroyed whilst 800 others needed major repairs before they could be occupied again and by 1945 the

Youden's Court off Market Street c.1930

wartime population of 22,000 had risen to 30,000 as people returned. It was not possible to build any new homes during 1945, but 200 damaged houses were repaired and a site prepared for 400 prefabricated 'temporary' homes. It was many years before these prefabs, as they became known, were replaced by permanent council houses on the Buckland Estate and at Aycliffe.

We have seen that the plight and extent of Dover's poor during the period 1900 to 1950 was exacerbated by mass unemployment caused by the world-wide economic depression of the twenties and thirties. An indication of the extent of this poverty is the number of extensive slum clearance and building schemes the town council, prompted by government, introduced to improve the living conditions of many disadvantaged folk. Whilst many Dovorians with happy memories of childhoods spent in the maze of crowded homes and streets in the Pier District and the Durham Hill area may regret their loss, not many perhaps would wish to return to those conditions. Whilst, no doubt, housing standards have been raised considerably since 1900, a Dover District Council housing survey of the district in 2001 classed 5,300 homes as unfit for human habitation. Obviously, problems remain.

Prefabs on the Buckland Estate

Chapter 10

DOVER IN THE 21ST CENTURY

At the beginning of the 21st century what was the state of Dover? Had poverty been eradicated by the Welfare State and by the opportunities for those from poorer backgrounds to improve their lot through free education and other government initiatives such as equal opportunities legislation and the minimum wage?

Economic and social information

In 1999 Dover District Council published economic and social information based on 1997 data for the whole district. In that year there were about 60,000 residents of working age in the district plus 25,000 children up to 17 years old and 23,000 over retirement age.

Unemployment at 5.2% was double that of the South East region as a whole with 50% having only unskilled or no experience to offer. Wages were lower on average than in the South East generally and Dover had fewer highly skilled and more low skilled jobs compared with the rest of the UK. Parts of Dover were among the worst educationally in the South East.

General Certificate of Secondary Education (GCSE) performance was in line with the national average, but GCE A Level achievement was below the Kent and England average. 80% of 16 year old pupils stayed on in full-time education.

The deprivation ranking of Dover District worsened between 1994 and 1997 with parts of Dover categorised as very deprived. The percentage of free school meals is one indicator of deprivation and at some Dover schools 50% of children were eligible compared with the Kent average of 16%. Almost 33% of Dover urban households claimed housing/council tax benefit.

2001 census

According to the 2001 census, the population of the Dover District was 104,566 with 32,598 living in the Dover urban area. Of the 46,260 dwellings in the District 72% were owner-occupied – a vast increase compared with even 50 years ago. Only 11% were managed by the District Council, following the sale of many council homes to tenants under the right to buy legislation, with 10% rented privately and 4% housing association stock. No longer do councils build homes, but housing waiting lists are still kept and sufficient points have to be amassed before reaching the top of the list.

This same census showed that 39% of people were employed full-time, 13% part-time, whilst 8% were self-employed. Jobs were primarily dependent upon service industries. Only 10% were in manufacturing compared with 7% in construction, 16% in transport, particularly port-related work, 14% in retail and 53% in agriculture, health, education and other services. Unemployment was only 2.3%, which was worse than Kent's overall 1.9%. In recognition of the economic difficulties caused by the closure of the East Kent Coalfield and the

125

effect of the Channel Tunnel upon the Port of Dover the District has Assisted Area status, attracting government grants.

Child poverty

The new Labour government of 1997 set itself the target of eliminating child poverty completely by 2020, but failed to meet its interim target of reducing child poverty by a quarter by 2005 from a figure of 4.1 million in 1998/99. What is poverty in Britain in 2006? Officially it is anything below 60% of the national average income. Apparently more than 10% of children from the poorest fifth of families are unable to celebrate their birthdays and nearly 60% cannot have a week's holiday away from home every year, according to the first official survey of material deprivation. About 20% of children cannot afford to go swimming once a month or to own a bicycle. This deprivation probably extends to being unable to afford going on school trips. Nutrition for the poor is also a concern with only the better off and responsible parents able and willing to provide a balanced diet. Providers of school meals are under pressure to make their menus more healthy and whilst free school milk was abolished during the Thatcher years (except for the under 5s), school breakfast clubs are appearing to ensure that children eat before their day starts as well as helping working parents under pressure. After school clubs, whilst providing activities outside the national curriculum, also provide a child care service for those working.

University students

Widely available student grants for university courses in the post war era have been replaced by student loans except for the very poor. The government's aim to have 50% of young people at university may be under threat with its introduction of tuition top-up fees except for the very poor. For the majority of students this means leaving university with a substantial debt to repay once they are earning a modest salary. What effect this will have when trying to buy a house and possibly start a family is yet to be tested. Already there is a growing trend for students to opt for a university close to home, allowing them to live rent free and work part-time, but missing out to some extent on the university experience.

Regeneration of Dover

In economic terms Dover and East Kent are seen as the poor relation of the rest of Kent and many parts of Britain. In 2006 there is controversy over the government's plans for many more new houses in the South East to meet demand, including 6,100 in the Dover District by 2020. Whilst many see a substantial increase in population as the means to regenerate the area, others believe that there is little point in building more houses than any local increase in population requires unless there are more jobs. Kent County Council's view is that in order to overcome health, social and economic deprivation and disadvantage in the east of the county a more ambitious economic development policy should be pursued and that housing growth in itself will not deliver the essential catalyst for economic change. An extension of the high speed rail link from Folkestone to Dover is seen as crucial. In the meantime as partners in the Dover Pride project Kent County Council and the district council with Dover Harbour Board and the South East England Development Agency are looking at ways to bring about the regeneration of Dover over the next 30 years.

Whilst extreme poverty in Dover may have disappeared except for the homeless and the vulnerable, there is clearly a problem, requiring different solutions from those tried in the past.

ACKNOWLEDGMENTS

I must thank most sincerely the following for their help in the production of this book:

Joe Harman, Bob Hollingsbee, Bryan Williams,
Dover Museum, Dover Library, Dover Express and
Dover Mercury for helping to find, providing or giving
permission to use certain photographs.

Sue Boulden for her drawings (see Chapter 4).

May Jones for meticulous proofreading and helpful
suggestions.

The *Dover Mercury* and St. Margaret's Players for providing
the cover photograph.

The staff of A. R. Adams and Sons (Printers) Ltd.
for the design of the cover and general help.

BIBLIOGRAPHY AND OTHER SOURCES

Bibliography

History of Dover by Revd. John Lyon, printed by Ledger and Shaw 1813

History of the Castle, Town and Port of Dover by Revd. S. P. H. Statham, Longmans, Green & Co. 1899

Dover, A perambulation of the Town, Port and Fortress by J. Bavington-Jones, Dover Express, 1907

Annals of Dover by J. Bavington-Jones, Dover Express 1916

Role of the Hospital in Medieval England by Sheila Sweetinburgh, Four Courts Press, 2004

Kentish Village of River by Doug Welby, Crabwell Publications 1977

Records of the Church of England by Susan Bourne and Andrew Chicken, 1991

Religion and Society in Kent 1640-1914 by Nigel Yates, Robert Hume and Paul Hastings, Boykett Press 1994

The Union Workhouse by Andrew Reid, Phillimore 1994

Handy Book of Parish Law by W. A. Holdsworth, Wilts Family History Society, 1995

The Life and Times of a Dovorian, Lillian Kay compiled by Derek Leach, Riverdale Publications, 1999

My Dover, Joe Harman by Derek Leach, Riverdale Publications 2001

The Victorian Workhouse by Trevor May, Shire Publications, 2002

Kent 1800-1899 Bob Ogley Froglets Publications 2003

Our town, Dover by Derek Leach and Terry Sutton, Riverdale Publications, 2003

Historical Atlas of Kent edited by Terence Lawson and David Killingray, Phillimore 2004

Other sources

St. Mary's Select Vestry accounts 6 April - 14 July 1836

St. Mary's Vestry and PCC Minute Book 1725 - 1832

St. Mary's Vestry Minutes Books 1831 - 1836

St. Mary's Town and Pier Book 1776

St. Mary's Poorhouse records

Lists of People with Settlement Certificates 1698 - 1782

Examination Book 1767 - 1794

Case Book 1802 - 1848

Admissions Book 1767 - 1784

List of outpoor, inpoor and amounts received 1793 - 1818

Work account book 1798 - 1801

Miscellaneous costs 1793 - 1829

General Accounts 1804 - 1828

Clothing Ledger 1793 - 1829

Inventories and disbursements 1793 - 1835

Governor's Accounts 1785 - 1811

Governor's Day Book 1795 - 1830

Governor's House Ledger 1793 - 1829

Governor's Work Book 1793 - 1798

Governor's Stock Book 1793 - 1823

Work account book 1802 - 1829

Weekly account book 1772 - 1775

Bill Book 1779 - 1789

Monthly account book 1832 - 36

Rate arrears accounts 1829

Guardians' Day Book 1814 - 1822

Guardians' Account Books 1798 - 1829

Minutes of the Dover Union Board of Guardians 1835 - 30 March 1850

Dover and Folkestone Union Ledger1824 - 35

Dover Union 3 April 1839 - 25 March 1841 Vol 3

Dover Union Out letters 1835 -

Dover Union In letters 1835 -

Dover Union Admissions and Discharges Register June 1835 - Sept 1836, Oct 1836 - March 1839

Dover Union Registers of Births and Deaths

River Vestry Minutes Book 1829

G. Ledger's historical sketch of Dover

Research by Charles Friend

Douglas and Janice Welby's research, Dover Union 1835-50

Bagshaw's 1847 (Dover) Directory

Brief History of the Dover Hospitals (leaflet) by G. Vickery

Article by Mark Frost 'The Boys' Ragged School'

Dover Telegraph

Dover Express

Dover & District Ancient Local Charities – leaflet produced by Dover District Council

Dover, a general assessment of its economic status in 1835 – thesis by Rosmary Piddock, 1987

Economy and society in Dover 1509 to 1640 – doctorate thesis by Mary Dixon, 1992

Poverty and the Workhouse in the 19th century; a case for East Kent – thesis by Jean Marsh, 2005.

ILLUSTRATIONS AND THEIR SOURCE

Chapter 1

St.Edmund's Chapel . . . . *(Derek Leach)*
St. Richard of Chichester . . . . *(Dover Museum d13783)*
St. Martin's Priory - a farm c.1850 . . . . *(Dover Museum d02217)*
Gateway of St. Martin's Priory . . . . *(Dover Museum d05613)*
Hubert de Burgh as portrayed in the 1908 Dover Pageant . . . . . . *(Dover Museum d15923)*
Refectory of St.Martin's Priory . . . . *(Dover Museum d28018)*
Maison Dieu c.1800 . . . . *(Dover Museum d02027)*
Maison Dieu prior to 1834 . . . . *(Dover Museum d02030)*
Dover Castle in the 12th century . . . . *(Dover Museum d03176)*
Ruins of St. Martin Le Grand . . . . *(Dover Museum d05473)*

Chapter 2

Museum model of Dover harbour and town in 1595 . . . . *(Dover Museum d03261)*
Buckland Paper Mill 1770 . . . . *(Dover Museum d02541)*
Woolcomber Street photograph by Amos & Amos . . . . *(Dover Museum d04916)*
Ropewalk and Herring Hang in 1821 . . . . *(Dover Museum d06448)*
Shipbuilding on the beach, 1792 . . . . *(Dover Museum d25362)*

Chapter 3

Dover Soup Society Notice 1816 . . . . *(Dover Museum d02103)*
River House formerly River Workhouse . . . . *(Jane Leach)*
Elham Poorhouse and Master's House in 2006 . . . . *(Derek Leach)*
St. Mary's Church 1814 . . . . *(Dover Museum d10775)*

Chapter 4

Casual ward of Marylebone Workhouse, London . . . . *(Sue Boulden)*
Woodchopping at Pontefract Workhouse . . . . *(Sue Boulden)*
Workhouse boys picking oakum . . . . *(Sue Boulden)*
Tramps awaiting admission . . . . *(Sue Boulden)*
Dining in a large workhouse . . . . *(Sue Boulden)*

Chapter 5

Dover Workhouse in 1935 . . . . *(Dover Express)*
Demolition of part of Dover Workhouse in 1936 with chapel in the background
. . . . *(Dover Express)*

Chapter 9

INDEX